Inspiring Messages of Hope, Courage and
the Power of the Human Spirit

WORDS THAT CHANGE THE WORLD

EMILY GOWOR

Words That Change The World: Inspiring Messages of Hope, Courage and the Power of the Human Spirit © Emily Gowor 2025

www.emilygowor.com

The moral rights of Emily Gowor to be identified as the author of this work have been asserted in accordance with the Copyright Act 1968.

First published in Australia 2025 by Gowor International Publishing Pty Ltd.

ISBN 978-0-6455734-9-7

Any opinions expressed in this work are exclusively those of the author and are not necessarily the views held or endorsed by Gowor International Publishing Pty Ltd.

All rights reserved. No part of this publication may be reproduced or transmitted by any means, electronic, photocopying or otherwise, without prior written permission of the author.

Disclaimer

All the information, techniques, skills and concepts contained within this publication are of the nature of general comment only and are not in any way recommended as individual advice. The intent is to offer a variety of information to provide a wider range of choices now and in the future, recognising that we all have widely diverse circumstances and viewpoints. Should any reader choose to make use of the information herein, this is their decision, and the author and publisher/s do not assume any responsibilities whatsoever under any conditions or circumstances. The author does not take responsibility for the business, financial, personal or other success, results or fulfilment upon the readers' decision to use this information. It is recommended that the reader obtain their own independent advice.

To those who seek,
To those who hurt,
To those who aspire,
To those who feel lost,
To those who dream,
To those who feel they don't belong,
To those who feel called,
To those who have felt broken,
To those ready to rise,
To those who need courage and strength,
To those looking for hope,
To those who love deeply and feel fully,
To those who want to thrive,

This is for YOU.

Introduction

"Never underestimate the power of a few committed people to change the world. Indeed, it is the only thing that ever has."
Margaret Mead

Having been a writer all my life and a self-help writer for more than 20 years, I am a deep believer in the power of inspiring words and how they change our life. The right message, when read at the right time, has enormous power to uplift our spirit and, in moments of adversity, give us that courage and strength we need to conquer our challenges and fulfil our dreams.

This is what I live for – to inspire people with the written word – and this mission is why I felt called from within to create this special anthology, *Words That Change The World*. My vision for this global project was to publish a collaborative book that shares real inspiration from real people – and it moves me today to say that we have achieved this vision. This book is filled with heart, depth, and the power to change a life.

The contributions you are about to read in the pages of this book have been written by 111 authors, myself included, from 11 countries around the world, from Panama to Portugal, Australia and beyond. Given the opportunity to share their message for humanity, each co-author has written a message of wisdom, encouragement, or inspiration with the intention to touch your heart and uplift you on your journey.

In the book, you will find messages about healing from grief, advice for mastering life, deep spiritual wisdom, and warm words of encouragement to give you a nudge forward on your path when you feel down and out. Together, these meaningful contributions from our global collective of co-authors form a book that you can keep with you on your journey through life.

In some of the pieces, you will also find a little insight into the story and the adversity that the co-author has faced and overcome on their journey, from depression and hitting rock bottom to surviving adverse circumstances. It is my heartfelt wish that these glimpses into their life experiences will be a beacon of light and hope for you, no matter what you are facing right now, to know that you *can* overcome your struggles and rise up.

Our recommendation is that you use this as a pick-and-flick book that you can open on a random page to receive the message you need to hear that day – like an oracle deck – and we trust that you will find the words you need each time you do!

The heartbeat and soul of every co-author is written in the pages of this book, and it has been and remains our collective mission to be the light in the darkness, the voice of hope, the reminder of possibility, and the encouragement for your unlimited potential.

No matter where we are on our journey of life – whether we are flailing, struggling, striving, or reaching for new levels of achievement – I believe we all need a little inspiration… and that's what this special anthology is for.

Words That Change The World is not just a book – it is a *calling* to inspire. It is not just paper and ink and glue – it is a legacy of heart, love, and hope. We wrote this book for you so that you may be uplifted in times when you need it most and so that you may do what you were born to do: live the extraordinary life you desire and deserve.

I hope that you will find within these pages the inspiration you seek today.

Welcome to *Words That Change The World!*

With inspiration,

Emily Gowor

Self-Help Writer, Author & Speaker

1

The gift of a lifetime is the learning that our perceptions of events can be altered by asking the most unusual question, especially when it feels like your world has collapsed. Those moments in life that can appear to be setbacks and disappointments offer us wisdom. They are designed to push us down the hole as far as necessary, until we are ready to try something new – anything – to get out of the funk. Recognise that these setbacks are actually a catalyst for growth.

By asking a powerful question and being open to a universal perspective, we can turn our darkest moments into our finest hours. When we are emotionally charged or feel challenged, we can be too proud or resistant to look for the silver linings and hidden blessings. But until we do this, we tend to keep revisiting similar scenarios in our life, until we "get" this truth and start asking this one question. It is then that we become free.

But first, it's wise to understand that there are only three things we can truly control: our own actions, decisions, and perceptions. Understanding that you can transform your world by transforming your worldview – your perception of your life events – is the game-changer. The first stage of altering your perception is through asking the most unusual, counter-intuitive question of all. Not, "*Why* is this happening *to* me?" but rather "*How* is this happening *for* me?" It is through this question that your perception shifts, you escape victimhood, and you enter the land of the victor.

Hamish Withington

2

You are not alone. No matter what you have been through and what you are going through right now. When you find yourself feeling lost in those deep dark spaces in life, when it feels like no-one is there to help or save you, those times are where the blessings are! In the darkness, you have an invitation to connect with your light!

Having a good cry is a wonderful release of emotions that have been trapped in you. Even if the cry is ugly, you will feel lighter and better afterwards, right? Once you begin to release what is stuck inside, you create space for the energy to flow more freely, in the most natural way for you. And it is meant to flow. From this more freely flowing space and energy, you will notice you have more clarity and can see the next steps appear for you on your path. This makes it much easier to make decisions. And from that, you can start making decisions aligned with your deepest desires, wants, passion, and purpose.

Once you decide in this clearer energy, the universe aligns everything – people, places, and opportunities – to support you along your way to achieve your wildest dreams! So, what are you waiting for? Release what no longer serves you. Reconnect deeply within. And let your unique light shine brightly as you step forwards and share your magic in this world.

Heidi Goodman

3

Sometimes you might feel small, ordinary, or insignificant. Perhaps when you grew up, you were told that you were "cute" or that you couldn't do big things or achieve much. But the truth is that being ordinary doesn't mean you can't make a real difference in the world. Ordinary people – people just like you and me – can achieve incredible things when we follow our passion and commit fully to it.

Currently, I am running an ongoing project to transform a village in Nepal. For you, it might be calling to raise a family or create a business that helps people. Whatever it might be, I know that when you put your heart into it, even small actions can create ripples that extend far beyond what you first thought could be possible. We often look at other people who seem successful or "special" and think they're somehow different. But they're not. They are made of the same stuff as us. What sets them apart is that they tried. They gave it a go – and that's how they discovered their potential. If you do the same thing, then soon you will be doing extraordinary things and pinching yourself.

The message is simple: trust yourself, follow your heart, and take that first step. Ordinary people can do extraordinary work. Every small act matters, and what begins with courage and faith and persistence can grow into something far greater than you ever imagined. If I can do it, so can you.

Barbie Cawthan

4

We all seek a love that our hearts long for, that we can truly call home. We may accept intellectually that it is inside us, yet we still turn outwards, our minds attempting to mitigate the pain of being human. We are led through halls of smoke and mirrors to avoid the thing directly in front of us – ourselves. Yet underneath the pain we fear to face is the tenderness of our own humanity, and it is at the centre of our *human* heart that we discover a doorway to the *eternal* heart.

Through the reunion of our humanity and divinity, we find an ocean of love that carries us at its centre, that is constant through any circumstance. When we turn away from ourselves, we lose connection to our human heart, and in so doing, our lived relationship with this love. The practice becomes how deeply can you feel and be with yourself, without guarding against your own nature? How open can your heart remain when things are uncertain? How sincerely can you turn inwards and not look away, instead sending compassion to what you find?

By befriending what we otherwise tried to uproot within ourselves, we come to find that perhaps what we thought to be weeds were wildflowers, with divine plans of their own. In allowing all of us to live, we discover a path that leads to a field of love that we can finally call HOME.

Lena Banzer

5

My words are for the beautiful soul reading this page. I recognise you and can bear witness to the impact of repeated losses on your journey this far. Along with your body, your dreams have been broken, and you are feeling like everything is disintegrating. I want you to hold on, though, as a period of restoration is about to begin, and the universe is going to be your guide. You can trust what is unfolding and have hope.

Even though doubt will consume all your senses, have no doubt that a hero will enter your life. They will say something of great significance that may well turn your life around. Life events will show you how to embrace all the different facets of the human condition. As you become present to your own pain and vulnerability, you will begin to feel an overwhelming love and compassion for humanity. As you become deeply present in your life, challenges and support will appear… but now they will be side by side! Synchronistic moments will guide your choices, and you will begin to see beauty, where, before, there was none.

As you give expression to your grief, you will open up to and recognise the suffering of the world. Consider grief the midwife, the bridge, for falling in love with being alive again. Your intuition will expand. You will receive guidance. I bid you to honour yourself with this gift of restoration to your soul. You will witness for yourself that sadness is love announced. The only way out is through.

Pat Armistead

6

We often define success through lavish possessions, extravagant lifestyles, or the pursuit of a picture-perfect dream. There is nothing wrong with this. It is, after all, part of what makes our world in motion. For some of us, success is measured in survival, the quiet triumph of simply making it through another day. We push forward through struggles that often feel impossible to overcome yet rarely pause to acknowledge the courage it takes. If only we could step back and see ourselves from a distance, we would recognise how extraordinary it is to face unimaginable circumstances while still holding on to kindness, humility, and hope.

Whether you're standing at the top or scraping the very bottom, you are already winning. Because you are refusing to quit. Some things in life are never meant for us to fully understand nor accept. They appear without warning, sometimes harsh, sometimes mysterious, simply to meet us where we are. Yet within their intrusion lies a quiet purpose: to shape us into someone stronger, wiser, kinder. Never let hardship, pain, or anger poison your heart and transform you into the very person you once despised.

Giving kindness even to ourselves can be one of the hardest things to do. We are often designed to mirror what stands before us, reflecting the world back as it comes. Yet, if we can remind ourselves not to lose our grip, we can choose to turn our struggles into strength, shaping ourselves into the very person we once needed.

Faith Monteverde

7

William Bruce Cameron once said, "Not everything that can be counted, counts – and not everything that counts can be counted." That idea has inspired my philosophy around what you are worth. With over 35 years of experience as an accountant, I've seen people with lots of money who are happy and others who are miserable. I've also seen people with very little who are joyful and others who struggle every day. The point is simple: money itself is not the issue, and it does not define what you're worth.

Now picture two overlapping circles: the left represents self-worth, the right represents net worth, and where they overlap is true worth. This model reflects the head, hands, and heart working together. Self-worth relates to who we want to BE (head). It is about our identity. Our net worth relates to what we choose to DO (hands). It's about independence. And finally, our true worth is about what we HAVE that we can share (heart). This is about our impact.

When these three areas align, we find balance. It's like baking a cake: you need all three ingredients – leave one out, and it won't rise. True worth is not about choosing between money or meaning – it's about integration. Self-worth is driven by our values (what matters most to us). Net worth reflects what we value (how we invest our time, energy, and money). And true worth is what is valued by us and others – the difference we make. The goal is to live a life of fun, freedom, and fortune – doing the things we love, on our terms, with the means to do it. Remember – your life counts.

Alan Jackson

8

Psst! Hey, you. Yes, you. The one with the passionate heart, the big ideas, the deep feelings, and the curious spirit… If you've ever felt alone in a sea of people – like no one sees the real you, then darling-heart, this message is for YOU. You see, if you're on a path of growth, chances are you've outgrown your life – your ideas of who you are, what's real and important – and along with that – your people.

As we grow, we crave to be met. Seen. Understood – by our soul people. So many of our relationships, though, are actually circumstantial. School and work friends. Superficial interests. Friends-in-law. That guy at the bar. Often, we don't even realise we've morphed who we are – just a little – to fit in with these earlier people. One small compromise at a time. To belong. It's an existential need, of course – this need. To belong.

But here's the cool thing. You don't need to change who you are to belong. You just need to shine bright, like a beacon of light. Because you don't join a tribe – you already have one. Bigger than this lifetime. A group of fabulous soul-friends whose soul role is mapped alongside your own to help you with lessons, and visions, and love. They feel your energy because it's already seeded in their soul, a knowing, that your paths are intrinsically, karmically linked. Only they can't find you when your light is on low. They find you when you shine bright. So, celebrate your colour, darling. Revel in your light. Your people are out there, looking for you too. Looking for your YOU.

Michele Peppler

9

When you experience silence in the chaos, it's these quiet moments we take for ourselves that bring clarity of thought. The whispers from our spirit guides, our dreams shining through! By taking time to find stillness in our mind, powerful realisations present themselves and the path ahead unfolds. The breeze through the trees, memories of the past, and lessons we have learnt take form in the silence of our being.

We can feel so lonely in our space, yet this is the time for reflection, bringing up and releasing emotions and finding clarity moving forward. Letting go and trusting your inner guidance can seem difficult, but during these times of silent courage, we truly connect to who we are, our true essence. Our lifetime of experiences are our own personal guidance; they are our building blocks as we constantly evolve and reconnect to all of the beauty within.

During this time of mindful reflection, we allow our path to unfold as we discover our innermost dreams. Trusting in silence, we open a treasure trove of love, peace, and happiness. We are all light beings on differing journeys, and we are never alone. The new lessons for our soul, the changes required for growth, come in whispers, the thoughts between the words! Shine brightly as you are worthy.

Karin Golisch

10

Did you know that gratitude and fear cannot exist at the same time? That's something worth sinking into. Before you close your eyes at night, prepare your subconscious mind with a sleep meditation or messages that truly resonate with you.

As you fall asleep, listening to meditation can help your body release stress and prepare for deeper rest. When you wake, you begin the day energised and positive, thankful simply for the gift of another morning. As you make your bed, greet the daylight, or prepare your breakfast – gratitude can flow into each small act. These practices align your thoughts with the right energy to meet life's experiences – both opportunities and challenges.

Gratitude also shows up in how you care for your body and mind. When you push yourself to move, even on days you feel tired, you strengthen self-belief and confidence. When you choose to learn about nutrition and apply it, you create a foundation for greater health and wellbeing. Each of these actions is a gift to your future self and acknowledging them with gratitude reinforces your progress.

Spend time each day in gratitude, focusing on what you already have instead of what you lack. Send a positive message into the universe and allow that energy to draw back the life you envision. What you put out returns to you. Begin your day with gratitude, because your energy is the source of transformation when you choose to work on yourself.

Karen Hepi

11

Do you ever get the feeling that there has to be more to life? More to life than living the same year seventy times and calling it a life? I am here to tell you that there definitely is.... once you jump! Experience the magic that happens once you step out of your comfort zone. When you decide to jump, life truly starts, and you can start living! Be courageous. Take the leap.

Honestly, I know that the fear of the unknown is very real. What is stopping you from making that jump? Are you afraid of falling? Falling is part of the magic. Yes, there may be a few bumps and bruises, and when you dust yourself off, you will feel more alive than ever. You realise that it wasn't that scary, and instead of falling, you learnt to fly. When you are standing at the edge ready to jump... the sun shines that little bit brighter, and the view will take your breath away. It will give you the much-needed perspective on the leap you are about to take, and you will find the different puzzle pieces you need to get you unstuck.

Chances are that one day you will regret *not* taking that leap. But I do know that you will never regret jumping towards the magic, towards your potential, towards the life you yearn for when you close your eyes. To truly live this life, you have to be courageous. You must jump!

Maryke Prinsloo

12

Darling-heart, don't you see? You're no accident. Breathed from the creator's heart! Lovingly formed, sung into being. Unable to be replicated nor replaced. Chosen. Destined. Blessed. Sacredly designed precisely where eternity touches time. Legacy wrapped in love – the essence of you, a beautifully stitched tapestry, carrying heaven's fingerprints. A divinely orchestrated harmonic symphony, resonating your unique love-song.

Dreams within. The light you shine. Birthed for this precise moment. Your existence isn't random. Your pain and burdens have purpose. You're not too much. Graveyards of broken dreams see bones resurrected. Hope has a name! The great cloud of witnesses above and alongside champion you on – to conquer, redeem, unfold mystery, and discover new tribes. Allow your dreams to shine. Only you can fulfil this extraordinary journey. Your sacred heartbeat's melody eternally echoing your unique heart-song.

Follow the saviour's calm, still whisper; come as you are. The true north star beckons – rhythm, timing, and destiny written in your soul, tapestries intricately woven through the great artist who etched your DNA. Walk boldly. Live fully. Grace overflows weakness, reflecting the love that made you. Never doubt that you matter significantly. Unlock the gifts embedded in you through singing your song. Inhaling peace, the fragrance of His love. Healing lies here. Run your race. Uniquely precious, perfectly-imperfect. Clothed with joy, strength, and dignity, laughing without fear of the future. Striving the finish line. Dancing the songs written for you! Shalom.

Vonny Mullins

13

I see you navigating a world that feels heavy. In a home with criticism, blame, abuse, and alcoholism. You've created armour around you, built walls and barriers to keep you safe, but that's disconnected you from your heart, your softness, and your kindness. You feel alone and question where you belong, and you live with fear lingering beneath the surface. I see you stepping into that protective, masculine energy, because to survive, you must. I see your strength, courage, and determination.

You made a decision – not to repeat patterns of judgement, violence, and addiction. You believe there's more and choosing a different path is possible. You choose growth, positivity, and self-discovery. And while trying your best, you will break down. You will burn out. You will crumble to your knees. But that is not the end. It is the beginning. In the breaking, the armour will fall away, and you will remember what was always within you: your softness, your kindness, and your compassion. You will remember the truth of who you are and what guides you.

Through this you will share your gifts with the world. You know there is more for everyone. Keep going. You're not broken; you are becoming whole. Get to know yourself. Love yourself. Believe in yourself. Trust yourself. Love yourself so deeply that you feel the freedom to choose your own path. The freedom to walk away from anything that does not serve you. You are worth it. Always.

Kim Guthrie

14

Finding self-worth is not about fixing yourself – it's about remembering that you were never broken. You are becoming. Within you lies a profound intelligence, a radiant truth: you are enough. More than enough – you are divine. When you see yourself through the eyes of compassion instead of through eyes of criticism, everything shifts. Stress softens, energy returns, sleep deepens, and old patterns begin to dissolve. This isn't magic – it's biology.

Your body, mind, and spirit are always responding to how you feel about yourself. Many of us grew up chasing approval, performing and pleasing because we didn't know how to source love from within. Healing brings us home. We remember our worth was never up for debate. We stop chasing validation and learn to affirm ourselves. Self-perception is not just a mindset – it is a force that shapes your health and your life. When you believe you are unworthy, your body contracts. When you remember your value, your heart opens, your vitality glows.

Compassion calms the nervous system. Love rewires the brain. Acceptance dissolves tension. This is true power – not ego-driven, but soul-aligned. The goal has never been perfection; it is integration. Body, mind, and soul in harmony, no longer outsourcing worth but living anchored in love and guided by wisdom. And when we rise in this way, the world rises with us. Families heal, relationships soften, communities shift. This is your invitation: to choose compassion, to live in self-love, and to embody the freedom and power that have always been yours.

Maureen Callister

15

Life can fall apart in a single breath. One morning you wake up as someone's partner, certain of tomorrow. By nightfall, the world is unrecognisable. The bed is cold. You feel broken beyond repair. The silence has weight. You collapse to the floor, wondering how you'll ever stand again. You replay every memory, desperate for answers, carrying a shame that was never yours to hold. You don't want to tell anyone. How could you? The pity, the questions, the sideways looks – it feels easier to stay quiet. But his leaving was not your fault. His absence cannot erase your worth. His choices do not decide who you are.

The grief hurts physically. For a while, you stay there, curled up on the floor, everything aching. And then, somehow, you rise. Maybe just to make coffee. Maybe to step outside for air. Listen to music, sing a song. Take small steps, uneven ones. But they count. Each one whispers what you'd forgotten – you can do this; you are stronger than you think. The pain doesn't leave, but you carry it differently. You bend, but you do not break. You grow around the cracks. Slowly, you rebuild. Not into who you once were, but into someone braver, stronger, wiser.

Deep inside, every woman carries a truth: she is worthy, and able to rise, even when she thought she couldn't. Your worth has never depended on who stays or who leaves. It's always been yours. You can and you will be strong again. Keep moving. Keep breathing. Keep loving. Believe you are, and always will be, worthy.

Nicole Masseque

16

To the lost souls who are living with an unknown, those who are feeling stuck, confused, disillusioned, and hopeless: you want clarity. I understand you. We may never get the answers that we seek and that it is a discombobulating space to live in. You could be seeking clarity around what has happened to a missing loved one or the full story behind a traumatic event, piecing together your fragmented memories. Life can be difficult when you are stuck in this space. I get it.

What I can tell you is that you are stronger and mightier than the perpetrators of your trauma. You will prevail. Do not become numb. Allow yourself to feel your feelings; let your tears flow without shame, and do not pretend to be happy when you are not. Happiness is a feeling to genuinely have, not for you to masquerade in, helping others feel comfortable.

When you do not feel all that you need to feel, you abandon yourself. Be gentle. Take all the time to heal from the unknown. Be authentically you. Allow yourself to be vulnerable. Be real to truly heal. Believe in hope. Not that you'll get the answers that you seek, this may not happen, but to find peace within yourself. Your life does not have to be tied to the perpetrators that caused you pain. Show them how authentic and strong you really are. You will prevail.

Kellie-Ann Smith

17

I know that life does not always deal us the cards we hoped for. Sometimes it feels like we're knocked down again and again, and the weight of it all tempts us to stay on the ground. But I want you all to read and take this in clearly: you are stronger than you think. The scars you carry are not signs of defeat but rather proof that you have endured, that you are still standing even when the storms tried to break you. So be proud of your scars.

You may not see it right away, but every challenge has shaped you into someone capable of more than what you were yesterday. Each stumble teaches us resilience, each loss creates room for us to grow, and each setback whispers in your heart that you still have another chance waiting ahead of you. I promise you this, the pain that once felt unbearable can become the very fuel that pushes you toward your ultimate purpose.

We cannot always choose what life throws at us, but we can choose how we rise. And when you choose to rise, no matter how slowly, and no matter how bruised, you step into the unstoppable truth of who you truly are. You are not finished; you are becoming, and what waits for you beyond the struggle is not just survival, but success that will taste all the sweeter because you earned it.

Ed Breedveld

18

Grief is not the price of love. It is the ultimate expression of love in all its rawness. It cracks you open, leaving you vulnerable with no place to hide. In the days immediately following a loved one dying it is imperative that you embrace that rawness and honour your pain by acknowledging the role you have played in each other's lives. Initial emotions can be overwhelming. Please have compassion for yourself at this time as you come to accept your life has changed irreversibly in their absence.

You will have friends, family, and community offering condolences and support in a variety of ways. You may also find some, for various reasons, are unable to be there for you. Please do not judge them or yourself. There are times you will embrace the support with open arms and other times you will want to be left alone. Be honest and tell people how you feel, knowing that "Yes, thank you" and "No, thank you" are both valid responses. People who love you will understand.

As time passes you will notice there is nothing linear about your grief. Like the ocean, the tides of emotion will come and go, sometimes crashing with devastating force and other times gently lapping as you lovingly recall or share a favourite memory. You will slowly integrate the absence of your loved one and transform into a new way of being in this world. Remember you are not broken, nor does your grief define you. Let your heart open and allow your grief to be the doorway to love, life, and joy.

Myrah Moon

19

I see you, I hear you, and I acknowledge you. The challenges you have endured, the journey you have walked, the adversities you've gone through, the doubts and fears that have held you back. I see you, I hear you, and I acknowledge you. The love in your heart, the kindness in your smile, the passion in your belly, the joy in your eyes, the vision in your soul.

I see you, I hear you, and I acknowledge you. Your life is worth living. Not just surviving but thriving. Humanity needs YOU. You are worth it. Know that you are not alone. Know that you have everything within you to make it through this time and all experiences to come. Know that you are worthy of this life. This world needs you. This lifetime needs you. Find that one next step towards the next version of you that you know is there ready to go. Feel into your heart, feel that light. Your soul knows the way.

When you feel yourself in those challenging moments, when you feel yourself in that hole, swirling around in the emotional waves, when your light feels dim, when your heart feels low, I invite you to slow down, take a deep breath in – as you exhale, hold yourself and say – *I see you* – pause – another deep breath in – exhale and say – *I hear you* – pause – another deep breath in – exhale and say – *I acknowledge you*. From my heart to yours, I see you, I hear you, and I acknowledge you. Namaste.

Shanelle Anderson-Cooper

20

Is it time for your daily check-up from the neck up? One lesson that I have discovered from a very full life is that real success comes from taking a step back and observing your thoughts. For me, this means that even before I get out of bed, I do a mental vitamin check-up from the neck up, starting with Vitamin A: *attitude*. I ask myself, "What is my attitude going to be today?" We all have a choice, negative or positive. I choose positive and my day is often great with positive energy flowing around me. There is little difference in people; the big difference is attitude, whether it is negative or positive. You make the choice!

Next is Vitamin B: *belief*. What are you believing in for the day ahead? It's about making conscious choices about who you are. To believe in yourself and know that you can achieve whatever you desire. Your belief determines your reality. Tell yourself you are a great person. It's important to believe in yourself as you are the creator of your own world. Have faith in yourself. You are truly an amazing person!

Finally, we have Vitamin C: *courage*. Having courage is working on self-confidence which grows from the inside. Start digging deeper inside yourself and find that inner confidence and bring it to life. Nothing will change if you do not. Dare to be different. Have courage. You were born for a purpose. You are unique! Now is the time to step up and be accountable. Your future is in your hands!

Angelika Jankovic

21

I see you, and there is nothing wrong with you. You are uniquely exquisite, and only you can offer that essence to the world. They say life is precious. We are in awe of a newborn baby, yet somewhere along the way we forget that we were once that new life, that our life is still precious. For decades, I didn't believe this and held the notion that I was somehow faulty and just didn't belong.

At times the pain can engulf you, trying to squeeze the life out of you to the point of not wanting to exist. Reflecting on that time, I am amused by the elegance of life and the breadcrumbs that trail us back to ourselves if we choose to explore. You see we're not meant to simply exist, as many of us do when we become overwhelmed with life. You are meant to LIVE! To feel alive, lavish in the beauty and wonder of the world, and connect through our genuine unique encoding that touches others in ways only your signature frequency can, whether through love, service, laughter, tears, or creation.

There is only ONE you. You are not a mistake. There is nothing to fix, except for the outdated notion that you must change to be worthy. Take a breath. Feel that? That is your life force moving through you. The very fact that you are alive means that your worth is inherent in you being you. I for one love that you're here!

Trina Ghauri

22

There are those who grow up feeling as though they never belong, standing on the edges, and wondering what is wrong with them. The pain of being unseen and silenced becomes a heavy burden to bear. Yet, even in that silence, a quiet strength can be found, and resilience is born – not the loud or obvious kind, but the steady inner strength and determination to push forward when belonging feels out of reach. It is a confidence that often hides beneath layers of doubt, yet it endures.

How we manifest this strength is up to us, and maybe embracing our personal style and appearance can reflect our inner resilience and identity. Instead of shying away from who we really are, we can take pride in how we present ourselves to the world. Our personal style and appearance can be a powerful tool of expression, not for vanity, but as a reflection of who we are. When we dress in a way that aligns with our spirit, we do not just look good, we feel empowered. Our style tells a story, and your story deserves to be seen and heard.

Let your life be your loudest outfit. Let your faith be your finest accessory. Let your resilience be your signature look. You don't have to wait to feel worthy, you don't have to wait to be perfect, you just must show up in truth, in courage, in love. Step forward, shine bright. The world needs the miracle that is you, because you were never meant to hide; you were born to radiate.

Veronica Jackson

23

To my younger self, I see you. The girl who often felt misunderstood, who questioned whether her voice was too loud, her heart too tender, or her dreams too big. You carried the weight of expectations that were never yours to bear, and yet, you never stopped reaching for more. Every tear you shed, every doubt you wrestled with, became a stepping-stone to the woman you are today. You were never "too much". You were always enough.

To you today, standing in the midst of your own journey, you may feel the storms of silence, struggle, and sacrifice pressing against you. Yet within those trials lies the art of resilience. What you are walking through is shaping you into someone stronger, wiser, and more compassionate. Along the way, you will discover bonds that transcend borders, faiths, and cultures – reminding you that kindness and courage truly know no limits. Reaching across divides will require bravery, but in doing so, you'll find belonging in the shared humanity that unites us all.

And to my future self, I speak with hope. May you never dim your light to fit into someone else's shadow. May you pioneer boldly, love deeply, and keep weaving threads of connection that unite hearts across the world. Your story is proof that pain can transform into purpose, and that the bravest thing a woman can do is keep rising, keep loving, and keep believing.

Dr Laraib Malik

24

Do you know how brave you really are? How strong you are? You are amazing for still being here after all you have gone through. I too have felt words that have bounced off walls and have knocked me down. To try to take up as little space as possible in order to feel safe, to numb out, to tell yourself it won't happen again and excuse their poor behaviour and to hope it doesn't repeat. Your heart shattering each time you hear and feel their words, and you question your existence. That is not love or who you are.

Oh, my precious one, you are worth so much more than the hurts you've had to bear. You are not the mistake. You have choices and need to be safe in your own skin. The words they used often linger long after the danger has gone. The sleepless nights, second-guessing, doubting yourself, and confusion that keeps you down. You are more than those hurts, so much more. You need to know you are beautiful, talented, inspiring, and loved. You're allowed to follow the dreams that were placed in your heart that only you can live. This is not the end of your story. Please don't give up on yourself. You are worthwhile and enough.

Life is a journey. It's about finding who you are. Discovering what lights you up from the inside after the darkness, and to grow past your hurts. To remember your uniqueness, your beauty, your magic. To love yourself, to heal and blossom and become who you were meant to be. Yourself.

Katharine Cheetham

25

In a world full of chaos and confusion, I am here to share financial wisdom, around being financially free. Being financially free allows for a more fulfilling and inspired life, meaning you can then focus on your life's mission and purpose. To really be financially free, it is essential to master the art of saving and investing.

True financial freedom is when someone has mastered their wealth enough to no longer be its slave. You have saved and invested your money to such a degree that your money is working for you, instead of you working for your money. This means you now have your time and freedom back to pursue what you love to do in life. It is important to spend less than you earn and invest the difference into appreciating assets like real estate, stocks, and cryptocurrencies. The more you appreciate money, the more it will grow in your life.

Achieving financial freedom is a journey that requires discipline, patience, and a commitment to sound financial principles. Most people put off saving and investing until their bills, debts, and expenses are paid. But the wealthy pay themselves first, no matter what. The concept of paying yourself first is a mindset shift that encourages responsible financial behaviour and prioritises long-term financial security. Don't wait for the right time to start your financial journey: the perfect time is now. Create value to the world by producing a product, service, or an idea, get paid doing what you love and are inspired by, and set yourself up a life of financial freedom.

Michael Gould

26

To you, the wounded soul, I recognise the pain you hold. The echoes of a long-ago abuse, the numbness, the grief, the loneliness. I remember what it feels like when your entire body and soul scream, and there is nothing other than a heavy silence, no one to hear you and rescue you. I have been there, too.

But I want to share with you a discovery that transformed my life. It was a simple phrase from *A Course in Miracles:* "I am not a victim of the world I see." Can you feel the truth in these words? They give you back your power. What if the pain and abandonment you experienced were gifts in disguise, opportunities for growth and healing? Imagine for a moment that you could fly and rise above your life. Look down on the events that shaped you. See the challenges you faced, not as wounds, but as the very threads that are weaving a beautiful and unique tapestry that is the masterpiece of your life.

Deep within your heart, a higher force has always been guiding you. You were never abandoned, never alone. You have the power to step into your destiny. Your golden path, a "path with heart," as Carlos Castaneda says, is clear and bright, just waiting for you. Listen to the call, take that first step, and become the hero of your own story.

Christine Maudy

27

We underestimate ourselves more than anyone else ever could. But what we sometimes don't see is that every challenge, hardship, and victory has already shaped us into someone with skills worth sharing. We actually have no reason to underestimate ourselves. The truth is that your life experiences create your life skills toolkit. Skills aren't just taught in classrooms or offices; they're forged in real life. That struggle you survived? It taught you patience. The mistakes you overcame? They built you wisdom. The rejections you endured? They opened new experiences. Setbacks sharpen problem-solving. Hard seasons strengthen resilience.

I've seen this in my own family. My youngest granddaughter spent her first three months of life in prison. Most people hear that story and see only hardship. I saw a unique bonding opportunity between mother and baby, free from the distractions of phones and friends and judgements. My granddaughter and daughter, whether they knew it or not at the time, were building resilience – and resilience is a skill. It is employable. It is valuable. It is leadership, perseverance, and perspective.

If you have ever whispered, "I have nothing to offer," then hear this instead, *You already have everything you need.* Every scar, every lesson, every story can be reframed into strength. What feels like a barrier can become the doorway to brilliance. The question isn't whether you have something to give. It's whether you're ready to see it. So don't underestimate yourself, because a lot of the hard work has already been done.

Britt Brennan

28

Imagine how wonderful the world would be if we all truly lived from the understanding that we are all simply parts of one loving, omniscient source entity. We would truly embrace the concept that lifting another person lifts not just ourselves but everyone. We would understand that no one, including ourselves, is better or worse than anyone else, just in a different place in their spiritual evolution.

Taking it a step further to include acceptance of the truth of reincarnation, we would recognise that we are never a victim of life's circumstances but a chooser. We choose, before coming into each life or incarnation, the circumstances and events to experience that will be of the greatest benefit to our spiritual growth. A deep loss, hurtful personal attack, or even a physical maiming can lead to deep empathy and compassion for others in similar circumstances.

Such events can teach us that we can get through hard things and emerge stronger, more resilient, kinder, and happier. They further enrich our pool of experience, knowledge, and wisdom, which enables us to give back to others more generously and in more heartfelt ways. The goal for all souls is to reach a fulsome understanding of "all that is." Life is a game with a set curriculum where we get as many chances over as many lives as we need to master each lesson. The key is to see others as part of ourselves in a different form and to approach all experiences from the heart.

Haley Jones

29

You were born into this world a pure soul, a blank canvas to be filled with experiences, emotions, messages from parents, teachers, friends. You have laughed and cried, and on the days you felt overwhelmed and lost, you carried on. You grieved, whether it was the loss of a person, pet, your dreams, health, yourself. But you kept going. You found that strength you had all along inside of you. You have that fortitude within when life seems insurmountable, when you feel buried beneath the challenges, and you could scream until you have no voice left.

But you can use that voice as your strength to say no when you need to, to say yes to joy, to what lights you up from the inside, makes your eyes sparkle, and your spirit dance. You were born to have a great life, to live your purpose, to love and be loved. Whatever or whoever stops you from thinking you deserve this is wrong. That inside voice that tells you that you aren't good enough, that you can't do this, is not being honest with you.

Let yourself be vulnerable, let yourself experience what you desire, and let that voice roar not with pain, but with passion and purpose. You are not alone, even though you may feel like you are. You are not alone if you believe in yourself. Life is tough, but so are you. You don't have to run from your past anymore. You've got this. Step forward and fly.

Maria Gallagher

30

To that person who is exhausted, dissatisfied, disappointed, and feeling like potential unfulfilled – you take it all on and you are everything to everyone and then get completely overwhelmed with life. You have hundreds of balls in the air, and you keep on juggling. Just when you get back up, you feel like you get knocked back down again. You drop balls and see only failure. And sometimes, you want to drop all those balls and just walk away… But you wouldn't walk away.

Even when life gets so tough, you know you have it in you to move through these challenges and create the miraculous again and again. You are the person who, many times, has no idea how to get it done, but you make it happen anyway. You have created a massive life, and you are the centre of it all. You are a rock star with power and vision and unbelievable strength to get back up and be an inspiration to others.

You're not a failure. You are a glorious miracle in action, a beacon of light and a phenomenal force. You are the essence of it all. You are love in action. Live every day as if you were born this morning. The past is a wonderful mess of accomplishments and achievement, and the past is in the past. You have infinite possibilities. You can have it all. You can do it all. You are peace. Keep being you; you are strong. You are powerful. You are a miracle for people. Keep on shining your light.

Brenda Homersham

31

Everything carries power. Your words, your actions, your thoughts, your choices. Each inspires, ignites, and shifts the direction of life in an instant. Be you, be courageous, show grit, commit to being a better you, so that one day as your life ends, you smile, and treasure the magic moments that you got to create and share. The magic of "what a ride."

Love deeply, be kind, show grace, give, be an example, play full out, share abundance, and don't quit. Be present, make mistakes, grow, encourage others, and find ways to enhance every day. Every word is a seed, every action builds character, every bit of passion sparks momentum and every thought takes you a step closer to the magical you. What a gift life truly is. When we choose to feel growth, or have fun and be grateful, we don't just change our own lives; we create a ripple effect, an impact that makes a difference for moments, years, and even lifetimes.

So treasure today, soak in the words in this book, speak with power, act with courage, break some rules, test your beliefs, and love without fear. This is your life, your moment. Claim it, live it, and never hold back. In the end, life is not measured by time, but by the magic we create, the love we give, and the ripples we leave behind.

Adam James

32

Beautiful, amazing soul, you are so deserving of whatever your heart and soul desires. From my heart to yours, thank YOU for investing in you. Have you found yourself always seeking happiness, approval, love from others? Do you believe that you will only find true happiness this way? I see you and I hear you. I believe from the deepest part of my heart that the greatest love is the one you can have with yourself.

You know who you truly are. Connect with you heart and soul, listen and follow your inner wisdom. You can then develop an amazing relationship with yourself. Are you saying, *That isn't easy, I am not worthy or good enough?* Those words are stories we can tell ourselves and they create deep wounds. Know that you have the amazing ability to heal. By connecting with yourself, realising what is important, believing and trusting, you can do this.

You have all within you to be the amazing person you are. Be kind, be gentle with yourself, dear one; you are imperfectly perfect. Remember, you came here to experience whatever you need to learn, to experience life and create a meaningful life for you and for anyone you choose to share it with. Let love guide you. When you find yourself having distressing thoughts or feelings, ask, *What would love do, say, or be?* Don't wait, create your love story, a wonderful relationship with fabulous you. Life is short. Now is all we have.

Jenni Albrecht

33

The mind is a powerful tool that shapes your reality and influences your emotions. Of all the painful things you've faced in life, none may compare to the suffering caused by your mind's interpretation of events – both by what it makes those events mean about you and how long it holds onto them. This isn't intentional or a conscious choice. For many, it takes years to discover that these patterns are often the result of complex trauma, which changes the brain.

As a result, you may find yourself living in your head, with an inner voice that becomes a harsh and constant critic. The mind is a meaning-making machine. Yet just because you think something does not make it true. Perhaps the thought is an outdated belief that no longer serves you, or the echo of someone else's unkind words that you have internalised.

Use awareness to notice what your mind is making things mean. If it is disempowering, reorient. Be willing to change the script to something that uplifts and empowers. When you use your mind intentionally, you create new thought patterns. The mind can work for or against you. To pivot, ask yourself, "What do I want instead of this?" or "What does my heart want?" Then focus there. Consciously direct your thoughts toward what strengthens you, not what diminishes you. Remember, doing nothing is still a choice – it's a vote for more of the same – and living with complex trauma, you may still need to consciously choose, again and again.

Tracy Knibbs

34

As Cesare Pavese said, "We do not remember days, we remember moments." This resonates profoundly, with the memories we treasure through life: moments with our mother, the day we embraced independence, and small victories along the way. The memories remain alive within us, shaping the person we become and the path we follow. They are not shadows of the past; they are the compass guiding our present and illuminating the future. Memories are the mirror to the soul, luminous reflections of our journey. They shine like a mirror, revealing every step we take and guiding us toward the life we are meant to create.

Every memory carries a fragment of our journey, etched deeply into our heart. Some shine vividly, while others soften over time, like whispers fading into the soul. Memories are not mere recollections; they are the sacred pages of the intimate story we carry within. They connect us to who we were, who we are, and who we are becoming, creating a bridge between the past, present, and future. By holding memories close, whether written in words or held tenderly in the heart, we revisit feelings, lessons, and wisdom whenever we need strength or clarity. They remind us of what truly matters, whisper guidance when life feels uncertain, and inspire gratitude for the journey itself.

Memories are sacred gifts, meant to be honoured and cherished. They tell the story of our past, illuminate the present, and light the path ahead. May we journey through life treasuring these precious moments, carrying them with love, reverence, and deep appreciation for the soul's journey.

Manjila Shrestha

35

You don't have to have it all figured out. No, not yet. And that's okay. The doubts, the setbacks, the detours along the journey, they all have been divinely orchestrated for you to grow and evolve into the extraordinary human being you are here to become. They are there to teach us something valuable about ourselves and the world around us.

What if I told you that life has a way of turning out to be exactly how you imagined it or better? Just not when you want it, or not at your pace – but at its own perfect timing. Perfect, as it is right now. You are exactly where you need to be at this very moment; and all is well. As empty, discouraged, and lost as you may feel, sit with it. Be curious, explore, and rediscover yourself in the darkest avenues of life itself: right here, right now. Heal in loving yourself so deeply, trusting that life will unfold naturally and beautifully before your own eyes.

You are never alone. You are guided by a force greater than yourself, the powerful force that lies within each and every one of us. I know how it feels to be where you are right now, and I also know that you will be fine. Because, what if I told you… you are the creator of your life! So, hang in there, dear. I promise it will be worth the wait, the tears, and the frustration. I promise and I love you!

Alexandra Lange Bernal

36

There is always light, even in the darkest moments of your life – sometimes it's a faint glimmer in the distance and your inner voice saying to you, deep down, to hold on for just one more day. Hope doesn't erase the pain of grief, loss, and darkness of multiple miscarriages and infertility, but it gently threads a light through your darkness. You might have gone from feeling joy and then to deep sorrow. Trust me though, there will be a glimmer of hope during the deep grief, despite not getting the happy ending yet.

Your heart might feel broken into a million pieces, and you feel this deep pain of longing for your angel babies to be here. There is always hope, regardless of the outcome you find yourself in. Grief is just a doorway to what you love most. This journey of life teaches you resilience, bravery, strength, and hope for what's to come. Soon you will realise that you are stronger than you thought, and you will get through this season, despite life bringing you grief and heartbreak that feels unbearable. These feelings that define you now won't forever.

One day, you'll move from simply surviving to living a life full of hope and purpose. The darkness that consumes you will become a distant memory, replaced by light threaded into a life that you love. So, hang on and show up, just one day at a time. Your future is bright even if you can't see it yet. It will be full of your dreams waiting to be lived. Hold onto *hope* that the best is yet to come.

Kate Taylor

37

For me, life comes down to four simple words: inspire and be inspired. To inspire is to breathe life into others through your story, your testimony, your journey. Every one of us has faced struggles – times when giving up seemed easier than moving forward. But your mess can become your message. Don't underestimate your life story; it might be the spark that gives someone else hope to hold on one more hour, one more day, or to rediscover their purpose.

My own story is filled with challenges: heartbreak, starting over in a new country, being told by teachers I'd never amount to anything. Each of these "messes" became the soil for my growth, shaping my perspective, and deepening my appreciation for life. See, inspiration doesn't come from a perfect journey – it comes from the depths we've had to climb out of. Inspiration isn't one-sided. Just as we inspire, we must also be inspired. That requires the humility and openness to say, "I need help," when we are struggling. Sometimes it's a hug, a prayer, a word of comfort, or the wisdom of someone who's walked the road before us. Vulnerability creates space for others to breathe life back into us too.

Ultimately, my mission is to inspire people to live with purpose and freedom – to steward their lives and dreams well – and my hope is that more people will recognise that their story matters. Big or small, it can bring life to others. Simply put: inspire and be inspired.

Colin Lee

38

There is a wisdom within that only you know. You arrived with a knowing, a deep connection to the earth, to all living beings, and to the unseen. You sensed it as a young girl. You knew how you wanted to live. But along the way, you allowed others to quieten your knowing. You doubted yourself, stopped trusting yourself, and the effect was you felt unloved, thinking you didn't matter and believing you weren't worthy.

I am here to whisper truth into your heart: remember the knowing you hold within is powerful and it will guide you. Trust what you feel, what you sense, how you see the world. Your intuition, your inner knowing, it is the strongest guide you will ever have in loving yourself and living a life you love. Align your mind, body, and soul with the flow of the universe to shine as one guided by your wisdom. Do not live according to anyone else's beliefs. You are here to live your life. Embrace the power and wisdom that already exists inside you.

The greatest wisdom I have learnt is simple: trust yourself, know yourself, be yourself, and you will uncover the true significance of who you are. So, to every heart reading this, you are loved. You matter. You are worthy. You are connected to a source of wisdom and power far greater than you've been led to believe. Trust yourself. Trust the wisdom that flows through you and the universe. This is your power.

Zenith Dunstan

39

When life feels heavy, it's easy to feel pulled in many directions. In those moments, the simplest act of self-care can bring you back to centre. Food has that power. Not elaborate meals, but the everyday comfort of a bowl of soup or a plate of fresh, seasonal veggies. These small choices reset your body, calm your mind, and remind you that caring for yourself doesn't need to be complicated.

I know you've had moments of feeling tired, flat, or unwell. You're not alone in that. But I also know that whole, real food can change everything. When you choose simple, nourishing meals, they bring comfort, lightness, and a deep reset that goes far beyond calories or quick fixes. Think of your body as your truest home. Just as you care for the space you live in to make it safe – welcoming and warm – you can tend to your body in the same way. Each time you feed yourself well, you're practising self-care. You are creating strength, building energy, and offering yourself the same kindness you extend to others.

This gentle act of care ripples outward, bringing warmth and vitality to those who share life with you. And here's the beautiful part: food connects us all. Across every table, every season, and every culture, food tells a story of love, belonging, and community. So, if you are searching for balance, begin here. Choose real food. Let it nourish you, guide you, and bring you home to yourself again.

Patricia Frederick

40

It's never about what went wrong; it truly becomes about what's right. Right for you, and your life moving forward. Take the steps. Feel the fear. The dead brown leaf that falls to the ground nourishes the roots for what's coming next.

That feeling of confusion, of uncertainty is just your soul's way of helping you realise that you are out of alignment with who and what you are meant to be. There are so many times in your life that you can draw strength from, all the proof you need is there: that you have what it takes to move through this, to emerge back into the sunshine and smile again. Everything is hard when you don't know how, but take it from someone who's a little further along the path than you are that…

Every single step forward is in the right direction. You will slip, you will stumble, you will slide, but you'll never see a sunrise if you keep facing west. Turn into the right direction and… Just. Keep. Going. Like anything worth doing, the days are long, but the years are short. You will look back at how far you've come, and you'll question – was that it? Is that really all I had to do? Our brains have a wonderful way of condensing and smoothing over past bumps – why else would women give birth more than once? Rather than questioning your worth, know you are worth the question. When you ask yourself, "Can I do this?" Know with absolutely certainty that the answer is yes.

Di Kersey

41

There is one message my heart longs for every human being to know: you are never broken, you are becoming. I have walked through deep valleys, domestic violence, loss, heartbreak, and lived moments where I felt small, powerless, and unworthy. Yet in the cracks of pain, we discover a truth: even in darkness, the light of our soul waits to shine through. Every challenge becomes a sacred teacher, reminding us that no nights last forever. Even in the deepest shadows, dawn is waiting and the courage to rise lives within us all.

I encourage you to never dim your light to fit the world. Shine it brighter, for the world needs exactly what you carry. Our journeys teach us that pain can become our purpose; the wounds can become wisdom. The wisdom that transforms our lives is simple yet profound: our struggles are not signs of weakness, but gateways to strength.

We are not defined by what happens to us, but by how courageously we *rise, love,* and keep saying *yes* to our calling. No matter what you face, your dreams are valid, your voice matters, and your soul's purpose is waiting for you to claim it. You are capable of creating a life that not only heals you but uplifts generations to come. So, keep going. Keep trusting. Keep shining. The world is waiting for your unique brilliance exactly as you are.

Anna Willey

42

We are all connected. On the deepest level we are one, with the Earth, humanity, animals, the universe, and nature itself. If we let ourselves, our connections with these other elements of the world can be an ongoing dance in which we flow. But the most important connection of all lies within. If trauma has occurred, especially growing up, in minor or profound ways, parts of us may be trapped in the past, inevitably leaving an inner emptiness in its place.

Emotions are energy in motion. If unresolved, particularly from childhood or teenage years, often due to difficult or confusing situations beyond our control, this emptiness will constantly seek to fill itself. It may manifest as forced and even reckless behaviour in adulthood, without us understanding *why* we act as we do, all to avoid our inner pain. The escape routes are many: addiction, infidelity, over-achievement, avoidance. When, in truth, these behaviours are nothing but a deep longing for self – a desperate plea to be whole.

So go inside, close your eyes. Relax as you gently recall the parts once lost. Welcome the fragments, invite them deeply into your heart. Breathe them in and acknowledge them without judgement. See it as a turning point to cultivate profound healing. Self-love is the most powerful love of all, so embrace it. When integration happens, reflecting who we are rather than us filling an inner emptiness, love for others will naturally flourish. Because true connection starts within, and it can lead you to the power of the universe.

Jeanette Cousins

43

So, you had it all planned. The perfect life carefully and thoughtfully built, full of hope and promise. The perfect family, the dream career, ideal home. You had it all going until, like the vase that was too close to the edge, it all got knocked off course. Suddenly your whole life feels like a ruin. The marriage failed; the career disappeared; the future that you had envisioned shattered, broken into so many painful pieces, and you are left staring at the shards and grieving for what was, seemingly beyond repair.

I have been there, where it feels like it is all over, it is all beyond repair! But I also know that the potter never discards the remnants of a vessel because it was flawed or broken in the process. No. The potter realises that those pieces, though flawed, are full of potential, so gathers them up and puts them back through the process and remoulds them into a beautiful vessel.

My message to you, from someone who has been there, is this: if you are reading this while standing in your ruins, take heart; be gentle on yourself. Just like the potter, take the time to listen to what each of those broken pieces are saying. They are full of potential, rich in wisdom and experience, vital ingredients to remould your life into what you desire. See where you are at as an opportunity to fashion your life the way you want it. Know this, you are not less because of the break – you are more! And the new you that will rise is not a consolation prize, but a carefully crafted masterpiece.

Yvonne Thompson

44

Life is not meant to be lived inside the safety of a comfort zone. True fulfilment comes when we dare to step beyond routine and embrace the unknown. Each moment offers an invitation to explore, to challenge ourselves, and to discover more about who we are and what we're capable of. The world is vast, filled with opportunities for adventure, growth, and wonder. When we choose to seek them, we unlock a version of life that is richer, fuller, and brimming with possibility.

A bucket list is more than just a collection of dreams; it's a roadmap to living boldly. Whether it's climbing a mountain, learning a new skill, or travelling to a place you've only ever imagined, each step is a chance to create unforgettable memories. Challenges may appear along the way, but those very obstacles shape us, teaching resilience, courage, and perspective. Every experience, big or small, adds depth to our story and strengthens our spirit.

So, don't wait for the "perfect" moment. The perfect moment is now. Say yes to the adventures that call to you, even if they feel intimidating. Push past the doubts, embrace the lessons, and celebrate the growth that comes from living fully. Life is fleeting, and each day is a precious gift. Make it count. Fill your days with experiences that light you up, with goals that push your limits, and with moments that remind you what it truly means to be alive. Rise high, enjoy the journey and, above all, never give up!

Lance Garbutt

45

Trust your wild heart. It knows the way to go. It knows how to lead you back to your truth. Throughout your life, there may have been times when you've been forced into boxes that never quite fit, moments when you've been told you are simply not good enough. Maybe there have been times where you just didn't feel like you belonged, where you were too much or never enough. But it doesn't have to be that way, not if you choose to trust your wild heart.

Take yourself out into nature when a storm is coming. Feel the wind in your hair, the promise of change in the air. Let yourself sense the raw power of the storm as she builds. That is you. You are the storm. You hold that same power if only you dare to trust your wild heart. After many years of silencing mine, I now see the truth. I wish someone had whispered to me long ago that the things you think are important – the must-dos, the should-haves, the endless chatter filling your head – don't matter. None of it is as important as living a wild life, free to be you.

What truly matters is finding the Joy. Fun. Love. Allowing your own magic to fill you up. So, feel into the deepest part of who you are. Ask your wild heart to take the lead. Don't waste another moment living half a life. Take back your power. Lead with love. And let your wild heart free.

Sandy Hanrahan

46

How often do you say, "I love me"? Loving your self is *not* selfish. As they say in the aeroplane safety talks, "Look after yourself first, then you can help others." If you know how to love yourself, then you can give your excess love to others. Imagine how you would like someone (your lover) to pamper you. Words of affection can make an emotional person melt with warm feelings. Positive loving self-talk when you look in the mirror is important to express self-love. Some people like to give or receive expensive gifts – jewellery, flowers, or toys make themselves and others feel wanted and loved. Think of your favourite gift and give that to yourself.

Touch is another important way to love your self. Stroking your body with creams and oils; wearing silky clothes that make you feel and look good; or a massage all give a heart-warming feeling. Give yourself a soothing self-massage. Smile and laugh more. Spend time with positive people. Enjoy nature. Give yourself a big hug. Appreciate the feeling in your heart and soul. Tune into that powerful energy and use it to achieve your heart's desire.

Unconditional love is free to grow and expand. When you love your self first, your love flows outwards – to your partner, family, friends, community, and around the world. Love is about choice. Choices you make have an effect on your life and change other people's lives. Loving yourself is the best way to feel better every day.

Allison Thomas

47

Four words that everyone needs to remember are strength, courage, determination, and resilience. We all have these, just waiting to be pulled out from deep within ourselves. They are buried in a place we never knew existed. Hardships and sadness go hand in hand, but we can all survive and endure these times. All that is needed is to just believe in yourself and inner strength will prevail.

Have faith and love you for you. Don't ever think for a second that you are not valued or deserve to be heard, because you are! True words can be inspiring. If they can put a smile on one person's face, that is what will put warmth in your heart and the confidence to do it again, until you then are able to make a group of people laugh.

Set your sights high and dream for the stars. If you fall, trust that your determination will kick in to let you pull yourself up. Brush off the dust and try again until your strength, courage, determination, and resilience make you reach your full potential. The power of the mind is not to be underestimated: it is a very powerful tool that you need to tap into to fulfil and achieve your dreams and your best self. When darkness tries to sneak in, remember there is always light at the end of the tunnel – and a hand at the other end, waiting to pull you back into the light.

Charlie Hovenden

48

Sometimes life can feel overwhelming. Expectations from others, a lack of certainty, being stuck in sadness, and the constant never-ending chatter in your mind. The stories you constantly tell yourself and keep repeating to yourself about life and your surroundings affect the way you see both yourself and those around you. Quite often, the noise within your mind can become confusing, leading to doubt, anxiety, and massive pain that destroys the quality of your life.

I was like this for many decades, shut off from my true self, my dreams and desires, and living my life how others wanted me to. It was not until I started doing breathwork and meditation on a regular basis that things changed. The regular practice of becoming quiet and going inward allows us to break free from our stress and chaos, let go of our external circumstances, and listen to the quiet desires of the heart.

Your heart holds more clarity than your overthinking mind ever can. When you start speaking and living from your heart space, you heal faster. You live freer and happier. The more you live truthfully from your heart, the more joy, happiness, and reward find their way back to you. My message to my younger self, and to you, is to speak your truth and achieve your heart's desire by letting go of past pain.

Phillip Manfredi

49

Your spirit is the energy of you – the vibration you send into the world. Every thought, emotion, and action creates a frequency. The question is not whether you vibrate – you always do. The deeper question is, *What energy are you vibrating with, and what kind of life is it creating around you?* Most people move through life unaware of the vibrations they carry. A heavy spirit, weighed down by worry, grief, or self-doubt, naturally attracts more of the same – repeating patterns of stress, conflict, and limitation.

When you vibrate at a frequency of fear, that is what you connect with. The challenge lies in recognising that your external world is not separate from your internal state; it is a mirror of it. If your spirit is unsettled, the life you create reflects that unrest. To transform your life, you raise your vibration. You become aware of the energy you hold and how it feels in your body. You develop practices that consciously lift your frequency – gratitude, compassion, stillness, breath, and connection to what nourishes you.

As your vibration elevates, the world responds in kind. You attract harmony, opportunities, and relationships that mirror your higher state of being. Success – whether it means love, health, freedom, creativity, or abundance – flows naturally from this alignment. The quality of your spirit is the foundation of your reality. By tending to your vibration, you step into your power as the conscious creator of a life that is whole, authentic, and deeply fulfilling.

Lyndy Saltmarsh

50

When you feel stressed, anxious, or exhausted by life's demands, remember – you are not alone, and there are simple ways to support yourself. Peace is always available to you when you pause and give attention to your wellbeing. In moments of stress, stop and find a quiet space where you can sit or lie down comfortably. Close your eyes if you wish. Take a few slow breaths and notice the support of the chair or ground beneath you. Bring your awareness inward and simply observe your body. Don't judge – just be with what is.

Allow your body to soften. Follow the rhythm of your breathing, letting the out breath gently extend longer than the in breath. This calms your nervous system and quiets the mind. As the body relaxes, notice the space that opens between you and your thoughts. The more you rest with each breath, the more present you become – in the only moment there ever is.

Here, in the present, you discover peace. Inner peace. No striving, no longing, no grasping. No questions, no answers. Just peace. And it has always been within you. By releasing the obstacles of the mind, you reconnect with what has been there all along. This is a practice. Create moments each day to pause, breathe, and soften. Feel the earth beneath you and return to yourself. In doing so, your inner peace rises naturally, reminding you that stillness and strength live within you, ready to shine through.

Claudia Ehler

51

Everything we look for can be found in adventure. This is a discovery about what's possible when we access something so often forgotten – a deeper sense of wonder and possibility in our lives, an awareness of this profound connection between outer exploration and inner transformation. Nature has a way of showing us. When we step out of our human-made world and into the natural world, we tap into a primal simplicity of life. Standing on a hill overlooking a valley, gazing out at the vastness – our minds naturally expand. The open road opens the mind, slowly marinating through the land, fully absorbing in our surroundings, fully immersed in the environment – this is where things start to make sense.

People reflect our humanity back to us. When we open ourselves to the world, we also open ourselves to its love. Unexpected connections with strangers deepen our understanding and inspire us to reciprocate kindness – a beautiful reminder of our interconnectedness. No matter where you go, there you are. The 'self' is revealed in this dance between what's outside and what's within.

When we focus on the experience of the journey rather than the destination, we become part of self-propelled journeys, where growth and challenge unfold for deep connection. They offer progress and presence, allowing you to explore not just new places, but new depths within yourself. This is a less hurried, more inquisitive state of mind! Journey slowly, live deeply, and experience life in its most profound sense. If you can't find what you're looking for, at least give it a chance to find you.

Codey Orgill

52

To the extraordinary and sensitive soul who feels broken apart right now: I see you, I feel you, I love you, and I am begging you not to give up on yourself. See, I know what it is like to feel small and inferior. I know what it is like to feel that you don't belong in this world, to feel cracked open inside, and to question your very worth as a human being. I know what it is like to feel lost, helpless, and hopeless in life.

But I also know two things. One is that deep inside your heart, you have a dream that moves you to the core. It is there, underneath your suffering. It is the calling worth living for and the guiding light that you need to turn your life around. And two, that you were not put on this Earth to suffer, but rather to be who you are and thrive.

If you give up on yourself in your darkest hour, you will never know the love of sharing your gifts nor experience the infinite blessings that life wants to share with you, from a career that ignites you to humbling and awe-inspiring moments where tears stream down your face – and that would be a tragic misfortune. You are not insignificant – you are *mighty*. You are not invisible – you are *seen, heard,* and *felt*. You are exquisite. So, love yourself enough to take a chance on yourself. Rise from the ashes, because you *can* do this.

Emily Gowor

53

Pain, grief, and hardship are a certainty in this life my son, my brother, young man. Amongst these periods lie blessings, and we can choose how we respond, always. Now, when you feel spiritless and lost, I recall that this passed, and the sun shone the next day. Teach this to your body and let it remember, because in times of suffering, you won't remember. Let your body remember and be willing to see the sunshine again.

The mark of a man is how he responds, reacts, and behaves when faced with a situation. Know, feel, and understand all you can, and simply practise acceptance for the remainder. Practice faith, prayer, integrity in relationships; connection to nature's elements often; breathe consciously. Let the body teach the mind through movement and stillness. The lack you now perceive in your outer world must not overcome the ever-present abundance within your heart! Realise this and actualise it because you do not yet know what abundant love abounds.

You will not know the power within you until the power is called for, and it must be delivered forth with a loving intention. When the inevitable situation occurs – respond this way. To evolve, surrender the mistakes of your youth to the universe. In time, they serve as powerful lessons. Create space for solitude to fulfil yourself with high-value activities. Intend to recharge yourself to an optimum so you may provide and give selflessly. My son, my brother, young man – practice gratitude for *something* every day. Emerge *consciously* from anguish.... Rise above.

Michael Bromley

54

As I reflect on the greatest challenge in my life, I believe in my heart that this is where I found the real me. If you are facing a challenge right now that seems insurmountable, or you don't know how you can get through it, know that you will, and you can. Run into the challenge headfirst. It is here that we find out who we really are. When I thought I had nothing left, when I felt tremendous responsibility and helplessness, I found myself. The phrase "pressure creates diamonds" reflects that our greatest challenge creates the most beautiful parts of our life.

If you feel like the answer eludes you, take a breath and a moment to reflect. In the toughest moments, we often surprise ourselves at what we can do, where ideas come from, or how resourceful we can be. I truly believe whatever you are facing right now will define you from this point forward. When you look back in the future, you will be grateful for what you experienced and see how it shaped you into the person you are today.

You are stronger than you know. Ask for guidance. Seek the support around you. Dig deep inside your soul. These moments are what define you. Draw on the resources that you need, but know that deep within you, there is strength and courage. You are made for this challenge. It is here to define your life. Be strong. I believe in you.

Anne Fry

55

I have been there. I know what it feels like to be split off, living one life on the inside and another on the outside. To smile when my heart was aching, to please others while silencing myself, to play small so no one would be upset or turn away. I know the exhaustion of pretending, of hiding my truth, of lying just to feel safe. And I know the deep loneliness of being so far from myself that I forgot who I truly am, unable to trust others, and worse, unable to trust myself.

What I have learnt is this: healing begins the moment you stop running. By turning toward the pain instead of away from it, you find a doorway back to yourself. Through embodied inquiry, through staying with what felt unbearable, you discover presence, truth, and authenticity. Every time you choose to sit with discomfort rather than abandon yourself, you uncover strength that you didn't know you had. Slowly, you become more alive, more whole, more you.

And so, I say this to you: you already hold everything you need. Your courage is greater than your fear. Your love is deeper than your doubt. Your light is here, even when it feels dimmed. The world is waiting for your true self, not the mask. You are here for a reason, and you owe it to yourself and to life itself to shine as only you can. Stand tall. Be the *magnificent being* you were born to be.

Yvonne Haeaefke

56

Words shape the way we see ourselves and the world around us. They can wound, or they can heal. From a young age, I learned how powerful words could be. Some words I heard growing up made me doubt my worth; others helped me rebuild it. When I later faced physical limitations after an accident, I turned to the words in books and from inspiring teachers for strength. Those words became my lifeline – guiding me to hope, resilience, and renewal.

Over time, I began to understand that the mind responds to language with incredible precision. The conscious mind is like a recorder – it only knows what you tell it. Feed it negativity, and it echoes that back. Feed it encouragement, and it begins to believe in new possibilities. The subconscious mind, through repetition, absorbs what it hears most often. And the higher mind – the part of us that connects to purpose and intuition – draws wisdom from these thoughts to guide our lives.

One of the lessons I share often is what I call the "French breadstick method." You can't eat a whole breadstick at once, but in small, consistent bites, you can finish it. The same goes for change – one positive thought, one kind word, one small step at a time. The words you speak to yourself matter. Choose them wisely. With time and practice, your inner voice can shift from criticism to compassion – and remind you that you really are okay.

Sheilla Ann Kennedy

57

Beautiful devotional mother, the one who is struggling to hold it all but carries on regardless. The one who feels like she's never enough but still says "Yes" to prove her worth. The one who loads herself with guilt for taking a moment's rest, and yet still pours into life in every moment. I want to whisper a secret deep into your heart: the journey of motherhood was never meant to be easy!

It's divinely designed to be your biggest joy and your biggest heartache; the ultimate high and deepest low. To crack your heart wide open so the purest *love* can radiate from the very core of your being. Your kids are your biggest teachers. The perfect mirror. A true gift sent to unearth your darkest fears and re-write the script of your life if you'll let them. So, when you're collapsing under the weight of your to-do list, or drowning in overwhelm, I invite you to take a sacred pause. Let yourself come undone.

Surrender into the depths of your heart and grieve for the mother you thought you should be, for you are not she. The truth of your love lies masked in the shadows of this performance. The truth is your journey was never about being the perfect parent. Instead, divine mother, you're here to live life intuitively, weaving the paradoxes and parenting with presence, opening your heart to the places that the purest love is born. This is the mother you were born to be.

Emily Robinson

58

You are stronger than you realise. Life may have tested you, but every challenge has forged an unshakeable core within you. The fact that you are here, still standing, still moving forward, is proof of your resilience and undeniable strength. Do not let doubt silence your potential. You carry wisdom that no setback can erase and courage that no obstacle can destroy. Stand tall, for your voice matters, your presence matters, and above all, you matter.

Every scar you bear is evidence of survival. Every lesson learnt is a sign of victory. When the world feels heavy, remember this truth: you are not defined by what has been lost, but by the courage with which you continue. Each step forward, no matter how small, is triumph. Every breath you take is strength renewing itself, proof that hope still lives within you. Believe in your power. Believe in your light. You are capable of more than you can imagine.

Your life is not behind you. It is alive, unfolding here and now. Rise with confidence. Embrace the new chapter that waits for you. Let your wisdom and your courage lead you boldly into the future you deserve. You were not created to shrink back, but to rise. You are not here to hide, but to shine. Carry yourself with strength, for the world needs your presence and your light.

Claudia Lopez

59

Who am I? Who is the one behind the eyes, the space between the thoughts, the silence within each breath? What if the final judgement was not of fault, but of perfection? You are already whole, already radiant, already divine. Beyond the noise, the chatter, beyond the striving, the question itself opens a doorway into the great mystery. Between the lines, in the stillness of not-knowing, the inquiry begins: *Who am I?*

You are not the mask of identity, nor the stories you carry. You are not your victories or defeats, not the sorrow of the past nor the hopes of tomorrow. Identity is but a fleeting shadow on the surface of the eternal. It is worn like a loose garment yet never touches the truth of your being. Let the weight of judgement fall away, the fear of what may never come dissolve. You are not bound by the illusion of separation, nor the vulnerable self the world names. Rest now in the quiet flow, free from the burden of becoming.

You are love. No path to follow, no goal to reach – only the freedom to shine as you are. The unseen current moves through you, the spark ungraspable yet ever-present, the light beyond sight, the spirit that animates all. Holy as you are, the mystery breathes you into being. I Am that I Am. All that I Am, you are. Lightning in a bottle, eternity in a glance – You are love.

Paul Morris Segal

60

The most extraordinary wisdom that I have learnt from life is to take time to see both sides of all events in life. If you've ever felt betrayed, rejected or hurt by anyone, the discovery of that simple fact of life will save your sanity. Some medical professionals will feed you their view that "someone has hurt you" or that negative events and people are just that – negative. Now I know with certainty that every so-called negative event is equally positive for us, and vice versa. If you feel broken and desperate, opening yourself up to that truth is an option to explore on your quest to heal the pain of anxiety and depression.

Life presents a beautiful balance of positives and negatives in everything we experience. Next time that you find yourself in a situation that seems only dark and sad, ask yourself where in that instant is the light of change, new opportunities, or who is supporting you more than usual? Where are the gifts in this situation? Reflect deeply and keep answering the question until the positives balance out the negatives and your heart opens.

The same applies for positive events and desires. Take the time to look for and find the balancing side of negatives that come with it. Seeing both sides of an event or person will calm you down, keeping you present and rational in your thinking. Not doing this will have you chasing fantasies for positive outcomes. That simple exercise will open your eyes to new ways of being the master of your destiny, not a victim of someone's actions.

Emilia Bruckner

61

You don't feel like you belong. You feel different from the rest. Being mistreated can create challenges that stretch our character. I want you to know, you are resilient; you are strong. Embrace who you are as a whole person. Look how special and unique you are from the rest. No one can ever take that away from you. I understand what it's like living with a disability every day, experiencing judgements and opinions, especially from the ones who think they know what is best for you. No one does, and no one has the right to decide what you do next in your life.

Remember you are the one that is living it. Other people's opinions and advice don't matter. It's all white noise, unless you decide to take it onboard. Listen to your own voice. You are your own compass and guide through your own extraordinary journey. No one else is living your life but you. Stand your ground and hold it firm. No means no. If people can't respect that, then they show their true colours and who they really are as a person.

Embrace this beautiful journey. I know it may be scary, but you will be amazed what answers are revealed when you're strong enough to face your own demons. That's what makes it beautifully raw. Be you! If some people can't accept you for who you are, they are not worth knowing.

Shenice Portelli

62

If you are living with the painful impacts of child abuse and struggling with the ongoing effects of expectations that families stick together no matter what, know that you are not alone! Our society places so many unrealistic expectations on us to maintain unhealthy relationships, to pretend as though nothing ever happened, to just get over it.

When a soul is crushed by those who were supposed to care, sometimes the only place for healing that deepest agonising grief of betrayal is when we are separate from the source of harm. In separateness there is space to take a close look at all the broken pieces, to choose which pieces don't belong in the authentic design of you that you are here to become, and to tenderly recreate yourself. They crushed your soul, and *you* get to choose what you need in order to restore it.

In the separateness, it *is* possible to find freedom and forgiveness and to heal the depths of the heartrending grief for those who still live… but chose to harm. Forgiveness for those who have never acknowledged the harm they caused. Forgiveness that frees yourself and does not demand that you put yourself back into harm's way. The truth is that you can forgive from afar, and you can hold love for the other without having contact. We do that for our own wellbeing, not for theirs. That kind of forgiveness is found in gathering the strength and courage to rise and to become anew, and the realisation that you can only change you. Choose *you*!

Nita Joy

63

Here are life lessons to embrace! You already have everything you need – so give yourself permission to do whatever you want. Don't worry about what others think; they're too busy dealing with their own stuff, trust me. There's life after high school and a wonderful world to explore. Go check it out. Try lots of jobs, start businesses, chase your dreams, and never stop learning. Money matters – it gives you great options – but it's not everything. What matters most is spending time with loved ones, having gratitude for the good and bad in your life, and remembering you're always exactly where you need to be.

Lead with your heart. Listen to it often. Your heart will guide you in the right direction, so trust yourself and your judgement. Try not to let the opinions of others offend you. Be bold, be brave, and don't be afraid to push back if something doesn't feel right. Break down and have a cry whenever you need to. Hug friends and loved ones often. After a breakdown always comes a breakthrough for you in some way, shape, or form. Surround yourself with people who support and challenge you, but want to see you succeed.

Ask deep questions and spend time in silence to find the important answers you're looking for. Face your fears, have deep conversations, and don't just go with the flow if something feels untrue to you. Provide a great service. Be fair. Treat others as you'd like to be treated – and most of all, keep dreaming big by living life to the max and doing what inspires you. Life's ups and downs are only temporary and ever-changing. So have a crack, make the most of your life, and always remember: permission granted.

Jay Harris

64

Reflecting upon my journey thus far, I can say, unequivocally, that loss happens to us all on this highway of life. It can sometimes feel as if our whole being fades into insignificance due to the pain of these events. One may even question the purpose of staying upright when all appears quite bleak, and the future does not feature at all, as the present is demanding attention – to the point where it can feel suffocating and overwhelming.

From where I stand now, I can share that it is during these moments we have a choice: to choose to allow ourselves to take some time to stop, breathe, feel, and evaluate on how we are reacting and responding to the loss being dealt with at the time, and how it can serve to grow us into a more resilient, purposeful, committed individual who becomes an unstoppable force for good – or do nothing.

Consider the moment of your conception to the journey life has unfolded for you with all the good and not-so-good experiences. You have captured these along the way and it is in taking that next step forward that you have a plethora of things in the toolbox to not only enrich your future life, but many lives whom you will come into contact with – be it a smile full of compassion or something greater. Doors close and doors open, and with taking the necessary action, it can ultimately bring forth a sense of clarity, contentment, inner peace, and knowing who you really are.

Jan McIntyre

65

Forgive those from your past. The people who have wronged you; the people who let you down. These people don't deserve your energy anymore, nor your attention. I know it is difficult. I know that every day in your head, memories creep in. You feel betrayed. You feel abandoned. You feel they don't deserve forgiveness, so you hold onto that bitterness, that resentment.

But forgiveness is one of your greatest powers, and it lies within you. And perhaps the person who deserves your forgiveness most is *you*. You may blame yourself for things that happen. But that isn't fair. Stop punishing yourself for how you let yourself be treated in the past. Find the strength to forgive and say *yes* to that lost love in your heart. When you truly forgive yourself and others, you also allow yourself to be forgiven. Despite our best efforts, we have not always done right by others. We are prone to misdeeds and mistakes. But when we open up the channel to forgive others, we also empower others to forgive us.

To truly forgive yourself and others isn't easy. It takes strength, acceptance, and time – in some cases, a lot of time. But if you address this forgiveness regularly, then, one day, your heart will feel light with relief. You will know the power of forgiveness because that bitterness and resentment will be replaced by love. When you forgive, you are choosing love. You are choosing hope. You are choosing *you*.

Ursula McCabe

66

There are moments when you find yourself caught in a cycle of fear, wrapped in layers that were never truly you. These layers, woven from old hurts and unmet needs, formed long ago to protect the tender light within. Sometimes the shield appears as anger, rising like fire to defend the places where fear feels unbearable to touch. Yet this anger, though fierce, is still a guardian, protecting the gentle essence of your soul until you are ready to feel what lies beneath.

The way through is not in resisting anger or fear, but in listening to them both. Anger shows you where your boundaries were crossed; fear reveals the tender places longing for healing. Together, they point you back to your true self, the self beneath all layers of protection. By facing them with courage, you soften the shield, transmute the fire, and rediscover the sacred spark that has always been yours. This is your gift, your purpose, the essence of your being.

And when you return to this essence, something beautiful happens. Fear dissolves into wisdom, anger into clarity, and what remains is love – steady, radiant, and alive within you. From this place, your light becomes medicine, your presence a blessing. You find yourself in harmony with others, with the Earth, with the cosmos, and with the great mystery itself. You are that love. You are that light. And the world needs nothing more than for you to shine.

Robert Grimes

67

If your world has shattered and you are feeling powerless and lost amongst the pieces, I want you to know that you are stronger than you realise and you will find what you need to rebuild your life. I know this because I've been there, many times. I've learnt that regaining our power comes from accepting our truth and giving ourselves permission to change.

Many of the pieces won't fit anymore and trying to recreate a life you have outgrown can be soul destroying. But, what if "picking up the pieces" isn't about restoring life to the way it was? A shattered world offers you a unique opportunity to authentically create a new life. Authenticity isn't about staying the same; change demonstrates your growth and can be positive and beautiful, even if it emerged from pain.

It's okay to take some time to mourn your old life, just don't stay there. Understand that it's not what you had that you miss, it's how you *felt* about what you had that you miss. Focus on what makes you happy now. Be openly curious and honest with yourself and the people in your life. Step into your truth. Give yourself permission to change, grow, and authentically reinvent yourself and redesign your life as many times as you want. When you give yourself permission to shine as you are, you create space for others to do the same.

Deborah Stathis

68

The philosopher Seneca once said, "It is not that we have a short time to live, but that we waste a lot of it." Growing up we are all given so much advice from the people that just want the best for us. Taking in the best of each piece of advice is how we get through the good and the bad. This can be confusing, challenging, and it raises so many questions about ourselves. The best piece of advice seems to be pure common sense, but it can also be the hardest to achieve.

When life puts so much pressure on us and we strive for the best, we want to be the best and we want others to be proud, it can be hard to remember to be ourselves and do what makes us happy. If I could tell my 16-year-old self anything, it would be that life is too short. Some people will love the real you and others won't. We don't know what tomorrow will bring or what challenges will be thrown our way.

So, do what makes you happy because, in the end, what makes you happy will support you to achieve and make people proud. Live your life in the best possible way. Don't regret your choices. They will make you learn, grow, and develop. You will make mistakes, and that's okay, because you will learn from them and you will be amazing. With happiness comes success; success doesn't necessarily bring happiness. Follow your heart and bring happiness into your world.

Melanie McKane

69

I used to think gratitude was something you felt after life gave you something big – the soulmate, the car, the job, the home, the holiday. But I've learnt it's the opposite. Gratitude isn't the result. It's the cause. Gratitude is the fastest way to feel joyful. It's the quiet habit of noticing what's already here: light through the kitchen window, a morning coffee, a friend checking in. One rainy afternoon, with my dog at my feet and music playing softly, I realised: this is it. Not the future I'm chasing, not the past I'm obsessing over. Now. This unrepeatable moment.

Gratitude doesn't deny the hard things. It doesn't mean ignoring pain or pretending everything is perfect. Healing still needs space, but gratitude allows what's good to carry more weight than what's missing. It's the lens that transforms ordinary days into extraordinary ones. And something happens when you live this way: life expands. The more you notice, the more there is to appreciate. Gratitude multiplies and creates fresh energy for living.

Gratitude isn't just a buzzword – it's a way of being that changes the texture of every experience. It turns "not enough" into "more than enough." It opens your eyes, softens your heart, and connects you to the truth that beauty and blessings are present in every single day – if you're willing to look. Gratitude has been my greatest teacher, guiding me from survival to joy, and from fear to freedom.

Kate Sanders

70

There are seasons in life when the ground gives way beneath us, when nothing feels certain, and the mirror offers back a version of ourselves we barely recognise. I've seen that reflection and lived that chapter, and I'm here to remind you: you are not alone.

Just as a battery needs both a positive and negative charge, we too hold polarity within us – joy and sorrow, light and dark – each gives meaning to the other. Without sadness, how would we recognise joy? Without the breakdown, how would we know what it means to rebuild? Life isn't always about being happy; it is about flowing within the contrast, moving between what hurts and what heals.

If there is one thing I would love to share with you, it's this: depression doesn't live on the ceiling. When life feels like everything is too heavy to carry, I encourage you to pull your shoulders back, look up, and move. In the movement, you change your state and interrupt that downward spiral, reconnecting back to the part of you that knows how to rise. So, when things feel broken, remember, it's not the end. The break might just be the turning point where you meet yourself not as you were, but as the person you are becoming.

Theresa Grainger

71

Trauma is not only about dramatic life events – trauma can be quiet, subtle, and deeply personal. Whether it is the loss of a loved one, relationship break-up, chronic stress, childhood neglect, or working in a toxic work environment, trauma is a natural emotional response to any experience that overwhelms our ability to cope. While the nature of trauma may differ, one thing is certain: no one goes through life untouched. Trauma can leave us feeling so broken and helpless, sad and lonely. Our world may seem dark. I know how it feels, facing many of life's challenges and being "broken."

Yet, healing from trauma is possible. It is not about denying or ignoring it. It is about honouring and integrating it and using it as a stepping-stone to something greater. True healing begins with the heart and the mind. It begins when we decide that we are worthy of more than our pain. I believe the greater your pain, the bigger your calling is. The challenges and adversities we encounter shape us into the person we are meant to be. You are not meant to just survive; you are meant to follow your heart to live an extraordinary life. YOU are here to shine.

An extraordinary life doesn't mean a life free from pain. It means living with intention, joy, and purpose – no matter what you've been through. It's about honouring the past while choosing to create a new future, like a diamond that goes through pressure to ultimately shine as a precious stone.

Angela Peris

72

Dear One, if you are reading these words, it is no accident. Your beautiful wise soul has brought you here. Your inner and outer clarion call for help has been heeded. You asked for answers to your suffering, the sense of feeling lost, scared, anxious, and overwhelmed. These feelings are magnified by the ongoing incessant noise and pain of the world across the planet. I feel you, I see you, and I know you. I am with you in that experience.

There is great news, dear one. Your peace isn't dependent on the external world. Your peace, freedom, and power are held within you. What I know for sure is this: we are intrinsically connected to all things. Within us all is a deeper consciousness that knows its unlimitedness and it is anchored in love. When you consciously connect and breathe into your heart, you can feel the calm. You can feel the peace return. The subconscious mind has a library of self-limiting beliefs that we can change and thus be more aligned to our powerful divine nature.

So dear soul, know you have come here to thrive, to ask questions, to remember the fullness of who you came here to be. You truly are more powerful than you can possibly imagine. Take that inner journey of discovery. Ask for help if needed. It's a strength. The world needs you! The world is waiting for YOU! It is time for you to fully reclaim your *power* and your *peace*.

Rosalind Sansbury

73

Today and every day, remind yourself you are living in these times with the purpose of bringing love to all you do and those around you. Remind yourself growth comes from outside of your comfort bubble and whenever you question what to do, seek the answer from within your heart.

Your precious heart does more than pump blood around your body. It is an accurate barometer to your feelings and emotions and knows more than your conditioned mind – which often responds from habit. True tranquillity comes from within. It is a powerful skill to acquire a questioning mind that asks, "What would love do right now?" In challenging moments, feel the answer from your heart. Try it. Practise noticing the difference. Feel the love, the appreciation for all that is, and the compassion for others. Science is now proving true heart coherence has a calming effect on your body, and when love flows from your heart, there is inner peace.

My wise parents used to say, "Make love not war." Many years later I am grateful for their teachings. In life's tough moments, love is a potent force for change, healing, and a soother of past wounds. Inside each of us is a dear heart that is more than words on a page. Our heart is a living, breathing epitome of all that can be in our individual lives. Now is the time to love and nurture yourself to allow transformation to a new way of being.

Jacqui Hartley-Smith

74

Don't forget to breathe – Take a breath – a deep, steady breath. In the chaos of life, it's easy to forget something so simple. When the weight of the world presses down, when everything feels like too much, pause and remember: you are stronger than you think. Obstacles aren't here to break you. They come to shape you, stretch you, and remind you of the power within. Yes, doubt will creep in. Yes, you'll question if you can make it through. But look at your journey so far.

You've overcome more than you thought possible. You've grown through every storm – more resilient, more courageous, more you. You've learnt to rise after falling. That is your strength, your superpower. And you don't have to walk this path alone. It's okay to ask for help. There is no shame in reaching out – it's an act of bravery. Someone is always willing to stand with you, to help carry the weight when it feels unbearable. In your darkest hour, reach out.

There is always light. Always hope. Life is more than pain. There is beauty ahead – peace, joy, and purpose. So, take another breath. Let it fill your lungs and remind you: this moment is not the end. It's a new beginning. Keep breathing. Keep believing. Keep going. You've made it this far – and that means you can go even further. Don't forget to breathe. You are powerful. You are enough. YOU are never alone.

Tracey Gordon

75

Stop! Stop!!! For just a moment, stop. Maybe you sense that something is out of kilter. Maybe you feel ill at ease, depressed, dejected, unsafe or just plain angry, enraged, and confused. Maybe you are even not wanting to go on anymore yet somehow knowing this is not all there is to life – I write this for you. Let me find my way through all that turmoil, unequivocally, to reassure you that there is more, that there is sense and meaning to all of it – absolutely all of it, even the very worst – and that sense and meaning is unique to you. Yes, unique to you and *for* you.

The truth of these few words presented itself to me many moons ago when all I wanted to do was disappear in a vortex of destruction. Take a breath. Think again. Take a moment to ask, "What if it were true that everything in life is happening *for* me? What if it is true that changing one thing, changes everything? What if it is true that my life matters?" Seriously. What would it mean that changing one tiny thing, like the meaning I give to something, changes everything? Because all things, right down to the invisible, infinitesimal energies of life, are all inseparably connected like an infinite sea in eternity.

Think about it. Breathe. Imagine. It means that your life, your very own life, your thoughts, feelings, and actions, really make a difference because everything affects everything and everyone else. It blew my mind all those years ago – it still does today. May you realise that your life matters – it really, really does – to the *entire* universe.

Dr Kim Jobst

76

You want to feel more alive? You want to align more deeply with your soul purpose? Maybe you feel scattered or pulled in different directions, all important, all vying for your attention? Maybe you just want a reason to get off the couch? A reason to keep human-ing. It can feel impossible, I know. There is a way. It costs nothing. It doesn't require any seeking outside of yourself for answers. No more reading of tea leaves or throwing of bones.

Here it is. I invite you to pause for a moment and contemplate your own mortality. Think about your not-here-ness. Your not-being-ness. Pause. Pause. Pause. Look around and take in your surroundings. Say to yourself: everything here will one day be gone. Every thing. Think of those you love and say to yourself: everyone I love will one day be gone. Every one. Including me.

Let this understanding of the brevity and fragility of your existence shatter you. Let it break you open. Let it call to the brightest translucent essence of you. Let it awaken you to the infinite miracles of experiencing life through the human form. Notice the simplest of pleasures; a passing kindness from a stranger, the humming resonance of a bumblebee. Savour a sip, a glance, a touch. The very fact that your days are numbered invites you to stop taking any of it for granted. Use death to come alive to the wonder and the power of this ecstatic moment.

Melanie Mayell

77

Your soul knows the way. Throughout the lonely nights, yearning for connection. Juggling your child's needs with your own. When grief rushes over you in a tidal wave. Struggling to make sense of a lost marriage. Dreams shattered. And yet, the love, the wholeness, the reality that has just been torn asunder? It's waiting to be reclaimed.

And your soul knows that *this* is the way. This path, however hard it is right now, is the one that will bring you back home to YOU. Your light, your unique, vibrant, authentic self. The parts of you that simply can't pretend any longer. Those parts where you've compromised, forgotten, dishonoured? Your soul is reclaiming them now. Trust this process, because the embodiment you've been yearning for, for something more, for yourself, for your child, is here. The light is already shining through the cracks you're feeling, even if all you're feeling right now is the cracks. You're coming home – not to who you were before, but to who you were always meant to be.

Your soul has been leading you. This quiet truth is rising from deep within. A homecoming, a becoming, a return to your light. Every experience right now is showing you how to create the life that was always meant for you – richer, fuller, deeper than your wildest imaginings. And in this becoming, you stand in the beauty, strength, and freedom of knowing that your soul knows the way, and you are walking it.

Dr Kathrine Harrison

78

There are moments in life when despair feels overwhelming – when the storms of solo parenting, grief, and fear press down so heavily it seems impossible to keep going. I know what it is to feel unsupported, to have others assume you're coping while inside you're simply fighting to survive. Life's twists and turns can feel unfair, yet even in the darkest times, an inner strength rises. With determination and a spark of positivity, it is possible to rebuild, to begin again.

Amidst your pain, remember: you are not broken. Though sadness can feel isolating, it does not define you. Time passes, healing unfolds, and slowly, light begins to return. Give yourself permission to grieve. Be gentle with yourself. Sometimes healing looks as simple as curling up under a blanket, sipping tea, and letting yourself rest.

Every challenge faced in adversity strengthens you and reveals what truly matters. Within heartache are lessons and blessings that guide you toward transformation. Change is not the end – it is the path to becoming a new version of yourself. With each difficulty, you have the chance to smile again, to step into a journey back to YOU. Choosing to embrace change, choosing to smile from the heart, creates resilience. Peace and inner strength grow when you allow yourself to pause, breathe, and trust in renewal. You will rise. You will smile brighter. And you will discover a stronger, wiser, more radiant you – one who is here, whole, and ready for life again.

Lana Arvidson

79

Have you ever felt trapped in a life that brings you little joy, where your soul feels ripped out of you? You feel like a failure in every aspect of your life? And you are over being told how useless you are? At one stage this was me, where self-sabotage, negative thoughts, and downward spirals ended up being my go-to.

If you relate to this, then I urge you to take a moment to consider a different perspective. You absolutely deserve a wonderful life filled with magical memories and purpose. You so deserve to love yourself unconditionally and be loved by others. You are a divine soul who deserves to experience the richness of life. You deserve to enjoy the wonder of the universe and, yes, you totally deserve an abundance of happiness in your life. These thoughts may seem so far from the truth, but you are here for a reason. When you decide to no longer tolerate feeling like this anymore, your inner strength will guide you. Trust me, take a leap of faith. You can choose your life's story.

Choose yourself, choose to love the real you that's hiding deep inside, choose nurturing loving thoughts, choose to fill your heart with gratitude, choose to believe you are worthy, choose to be there for yourself and others. Even in the darkest of times light can shine though. Embrace that light within and let it guide you. Hold onto uplifting thoughts, for *you* are beautiful. You've got this – take it one breath and one thought at a time.

Diana Hansen

80

God, grant me the serenity to accept the things I cannot change, courage to change the things I can, and wisdom to know the difference. These words, literally, saved my life. Trauma is a difficult thing to circumnavigate. It can consume you until you are living and breathing it 24/7. However, as I was fortunate to find out, there is a rainbow after every storm. The clouds roll away, the brilliant azure sky replaces them, and the golden globe of warmth envelops us. We can breathe again and be thankful that a new day is here.

My message to all is to learn to love yourself before anyone else. If you can't love you, how can you love others? It is not selfish to take time out for your own needs. It is a tonic to reset the mind, body, and soul, and it is very much needed in today's busy and bustling world.

Turn off from everything around you and look inside. What do you need to replenish yourself? Is your inner child still trying to forge a relationship with the older you? Let them into your life and become whole again. You will be much stronger for mending the fractures that existed and rekindling the love for each other. Remember, time heals all wounds. Find beauty in everything you see, laugh at the simple things that make you happy and alive, and trust that you know how to find the strength needed in times of adversity. You CAN do this.

Annie Chandler

81

The Big Bang story is about the birth of our universe. An eternity ago, every element of energy and matter within us – every plant, creature, star, galaxy – everything – was infinitely close. Since then, everything continues to expand and transform. We are made of ancient stardust! From that tiny and explosive beginning, the expansiveness of our universe is remarkable. Cosmologists estimate four to seven trillion galaxies in the observable universe, which is considered to be 93 billion light years across – and it is still growing.

Many in our world judge and treat people they don't understand harshly and with contempt. But imagine if we all remembered our original closeness? We are all related in this cosmic family: you and I; all of life; the entire universe. This calls for love and conscious connection. Humanity needs love, kindness, and humility, now more than ever, including to all of nature, with those close to us and with those whom we don't understand.

When we are confronted by ideas and people that we are unfamiliar with, I want you to remember that love and acceptance are the only way forward. It is the only enduring power that we truly have: to keep on choosing love and acceptance when we find ourselves facing things that we don't understand. We, everyone, and the entire transforming universe are miracles! Remember every day that unconditional love, humility, and kindness are also miracles that heal and transform.

Emme Krystelle

82

Follow your heart, it never lies. When you feel alone, always seek refuge in the pure and beautiful company of your soul. Listen to your heart; it will guide you with a clear, transparent, and precise message. No matter what you are going through right now, trust that you will find the answer. You are not alone. I have seen you travel difficult paths, and it has been worth it. Because every seed of love, wisdom, and example that you have sown has illuminated and transformed many lives.

You are more powerful, stronger, and braver than you think, and you have the ability to draw up a plan from a higher perspective. You didn't give up, you haven't given up, and you won't give up because that inner voice whispers the words that show you the right pathway, regardless of how difficult, arduous, or steep it may be. You are the light for those in darkness, you are the compass for those who feel lost, and you are the role model of resilience for those who feel defeated. Your presence is the essence that uplifts spirits.

Always, always listen to your inner voice that tells you, "Your presence is your gift of life." Our heart is the messenger that guides us through adversity. It is our life's partner in this earthly world, holding our hand to reassure that the Universe offers infinite opportunities to each and every one of us, wherever we go. Your *presence* is the *gift* for every being who crosses your journey!

Martha Bernal

83

A life-threatening car accident often activates a life review generating change. A close encounter with death can ignite a spark deep within that can become a raging fire. Gathering momentum, it burns everything in its path that's out of alignment. We can experience change in a radical way and it can come forward with force and veracity. In the moment of impact, messages from our inner voice can be loud, direct, and to the point. That night, after my accident, my inner voice screamed at me, "GET OUT! Get out of the relationship, the career, the identity, the current life path."

Whispered messages can come forward, like eternal truths calling us home, "Be true to yourself." The soul beckons us to rise up. When we are living a pale version of who we truly are, the sleeping serpent of our potential will demand that we allow her to unfurl, gathering her full power as she rises.

When your soul wants you to listen, the messages will come in a way unique to you. They may come as a roar to awaken you or a gentle whisper caressing the door of your heart. Words will be delivered to your entire being in a vibration of truth deep within you. It may shake you to the very core, or seduce you, like a long-lost lover. Your mission: always be listening. The messages will come forward from your soul-self. Be quiet and listen to that deep inner stillness where only truth exists… Are you paying attention?

Jane Gruebner

84

Breathe slow, deep breaths, feel your breath calming you as you breathe. Now breathe from deep within your tummy. As you breathe out, feel yourself releasing any fear, releasing any butterflies left fluttering within your body. Can you feel the calmness wash over you? You are a beautiful little human being; you are worthy; you are amazing; you are a child of pure love and joy; you are here on Mother Earth to make a difference. To share your love, your sensitivity, your amazing gifts. You are connected to God, the angels, and the spirit world. A beam of light that shines so bright that others will be drawn to you for guidance.

Don't let anyone dull your sparkle! You can do this. Believe in yourself. Breathe again and visualise yourself in a beautiful white bubble of light, a white bubble of protection. Archangel Michael, the protector, will watch over you if you ask him for help. He will be there for you, protecting you and guiding you to find your way through.

I want to share with you an affirmation you can say every morning to help you on your journey so that you feel safe, loved, and you can be who you truly want to be: *I am blessed beyond my fondest dreams. I am one with the creative power of the universe and this connection brings me fulfilment and abundance. I learn from every experience and everything I touch is a success. Thank you. What can I do to amaze myself today?*

Suzanne Fox-Kennedy

85

Watching my mother pass was an inspiring blessing. I was lucky enough to spend quality time with her before she emigrated to heaven. It was very clear she was taking memories and experiences with her, not stuff! In that moment, I became determined that I would lead a life full of peak experiences, which was a phrase I coined to define exactly what this meant. I use seven filters to ensure that everything I do meets these criteria: love, abundance, joy, self-care, staying present, spending time with like-minded people, and living life on purpose. Maybe you could use these or create your own filters.

A peak experience can be significant – like sailing across the Atlantic – but it can just as easily be meeting up with a friend or relative for coffee. The point is that it is something that you determine to do because it enhances your life. Remember you always have a choice at every moment of every day. Choose wisely!

I challenge you to start living life on purpose, with a purpose. Express gratitude for each and every one of these peak experiences. Notice them in your life. Seek ways to include more of them and share with those nearest and dearest to you. Start cutting out the things and people that don't measure up. It is very liberating! Your life will be enriched and enhanced as you focus on all the amazing things that you do and the people you attract.

Tim Matcham

86

True healing starts with forgiveness. As I reflect on all the things I've done in my life, I am so proud of my family and grateful for the love that God has for me. As a 52-year-old wife, mother, and grandmother, it's with an open heart that I share my message of strength with you.

This is what I know to be true. Forgive with all your heart, even when it hurts. Holding onto the past will not serve you. It's not easy, but you can do it. Just let go! Surrender! Who cares what other people think? Time is too precious to waste a single drop of it. Surround yourself with like-minded people who only want the best for you. Keep moving forward and never look back. This is your time to shine – so shine. Your blessings are waiting for you. But you need to let go of the old and embrace the new as much as possible. Allow others to stand in the gap for you, to be strong for you when you're weak. It's okay to have low-vibe days, but please don't stay there.

Pour love into yourself, fill your cup. Know that you are valued and loved. Time spent with loved ones is more important than money. Success is being loved and loving others, even when it's difficult. I pray that you find the light in the darkness and never give up on yourself!

Honor Turner

87

There comes a time when you step out into the big wide world, and it can feel daunting. Suddenly, you go from being a big fish in a small pond to a small fish in a very big pond. It prompts the questions, *Where do I fit in? What am I good at?* At times, the uncertainty can feel overwhelming. You will try new things, and sometimes they won't work out. You can lose confidence and feel the wind knocked out of your sails. But here's what I know: that is what courage looks like.

Growth happens when you nudge the boundaries of your comfort zone. It may feel scary, but every step you take teaches you something new about yourself. The answers you are searching for are not out there. They are within you. So, lead with your heart. Trust your intuition. It whispers, never shouts. And remember that every setback is shaping your strength – there is a hidden blessing you may not see until later.

So, when you feel like giving up, don't. Keep trying. Keep learning. Keep believing in yourself. Passion is your compass. Persistence is your power. And your work is your privilege – your gift back to the world, because through work, your purpose unfolds, your confidence grows, and your dreams begin.

Alison Pilling

88

Know that you have the ability to reclaim your life and rise above the dramas, even when you feel like a plastic bag blowing aimlessly around in the wind. A strong healthy tree has a deep-rooted structure to nourish it and bark to protect its heart and core. It establishes these foundations first before focusing its energy to the top. The deeper the roots, the stronger it will grow to weather life's storms, bending and standing tall again, without breaking or becoming uprooted. With each season, it becomes more vibrant and flourishes, with healthy branches, lush bright leaves, flowers, and fruit, basking in the warmth of the sun.

Now imagine yourself being that strong, deep-rooted tree. Instead of living in your head and thoughts, make sure your truth, beliefs, and morals are all well-grounded. Now, wrap yourself in armour to protect your core. Take pleasure in the small things, venture outside, be that child again running through the grass barefoot, carefree, jumping the waves, laughing and rolling around, blessed for what nature and the universe has provided.

Let your worries roll away and keep your eyes focused on what magic lays ahead. Embrace life's lessons knowing that with every passing season and challenge you become stronger and evolve into the person that you were always destined to be. Life is for living, so shine your light brightly for all those around to see, and enjoy this amazing journey called life.

Niki Rentoul

89

For all the strong, lost souls, you've had too many jolts from the universe, and it took a while for you to realise them. You've been in survival mode for too long. Burnt out, hiding under a rock from the shame and guilt for not doing more. You wake up one day, feeling empty, confused, purposeless, wondering: *What on earth happened?*

You've been exhaustingly angry, feeling the judgement around you like barbed wire, making you lose your sparkle, confidence. On the outside, you pretend you are unshakeable, while inside, you are weathering a storm. People are in awe of the strength of your walls and stay away. Use this pressure not as a filler of time or a fire to keep putting out, but as a fuel. Tread with curiosity.

Here is the truth. Past experiences do not define you; they refine you. Diamonds form under pressure. You don't need to turn back time to correct anything. You can reflect to find out what took your power away so you can reclaim it. Even if belief and trust in others have slipped away for a while, you are allowed to find the path back to you, believe in you, discover the gems inside you. You are always there for you. You are always in your head, so speak kindly to yourself and thank you for always having your back, even if you lose track momentarily. You are your best friend. Life is a trip of fleeting, precious moments. Learn to love the travelling!

Dimitra Mersinia

90

In a world that is often overwhelming and chaotic, it is easy to feel lost and disconnected. Yet, what if it was possible to rise above the turmoil in this stormy world and forge a path of calm and inner peace? If you stood up and showed your soul? If you let your voice be heard to share your deepest passions with the world? If you lived a life grounded in authenticity?

When you dare to embody your true nature, fully present in the moment, you become resilient and better equipped to navigate life with grace and poise. When you let yourself show your soul, you share your light with the world, and you allow yourself to connect with your inner wisdom. When you are not afraid to share yourself with others, without fear of societal judgement or rejection, your uniqueness becomes your strength.

When you prioritise self-care and self-love, your confidence shines beyond measure. When you stand up and show your soul, you are not just transforming your own life, you are inspiring others to do the same, without hesitation or apology, creating a ripple effect that spreads far and wide. When you allow yourself to be vulnerable and share your stories, struggles, joys, and triumphs with others, you are generating a bond of trust, connection, and community. When you treat yourself and others with kindness and respect, you are fostering an unbreakable force of compassion. In a world that values conformity and superficiality, your deepest desires and most profound passions are what makes you stand out. They are the keys to unlocking a life of freedom and meaning.

Bianca Madison-Vuleta

91

The speaking-out shift is now, and you are part of the movement of souls who are here to make your voice become the wildfire that extinguishes the old, ready to form the foundations of the new. We all have been burned by grief, loss, trauma, and life-shattering moments. As sensitive souls, we became casualty to losing our voice. I'm sorry you felt silenced. That your tears went unnoticed. That your struggle fell on deaf ears. That your stand for justice was ignored. That at times you felt tarred and feathered. You sat on the edge – feeling alone with a voice unwelcome… so you tamed it.

We all share stories where our voices were extinguished. But we shall not be silenced by fire. Instead, we will rise like the phoenix from the ashes. Our stories are embers that become fuel, not fury. We heal the scars and forge new paths. We celebrate the soul calling and capabilities that we have cultivated from experiencing the blaze. Our wisdom is our welcomed battle-wound. But our world is wounded. In the fire that ravages the globe in its current craziness and crumbling, let's welcome the opportunity for regrowth, regeneration, revolution.

Activate your voice, your inner fire, in story, poetic prose, songwriting, appeals, petitions, and advocacy forums. Lead a movement with your unleashed ideas, words, and profound truths that impact the collective. Cherish your conviction. Lead your cause. Let not the bird be silenced, for she has a call – to advocate where people and humanity thrive from the healing balm of a bold voice. Yours.

Janelle Fletcher

92

To all the old souls, the magic seekers, the constant learners, the curious explorers – please do keep being. I know you care, even for strangers who don't acknowledge your existence. I know you try to pull from darkness those who seem disconnected from who they truly are. I know your heart aches from giving too fast and too much. I know you feel, sometimes way too deeply for the wrong ones. To those who stare at clouds and find freedom, to those who can embrace the golden light of the sun and dance under the rain with a smile, I see you: you are magical, you truly are.

The universe needs you to dust your wings, to keep flying, spreading your light, using your sweet chant to awaken other souls that are sleepy and might have forgotten the miracle of being alive. Please look deep inside your heart, tune to your purpose in this life, and do not dare to look down or behind. Your energy raises above the disappointments and negativity that may come from daily life.

We need you. Shine your light courageously, especially when it gets dark. Your soul is the fuel that will keep you going and connect you with other stars in your tribe. You are not alone in this sacred work of illumination to make this journey loving and worthwhile.

Jenny Kjaer

93

The world is our home, but maybe you've felt it too – that quiet ache, that lingering question, *Where do I belong?* I carried that question for years, silently, as life moved forward. But part of me stayed behind, somewhere in memory, somewhere in the soil of a place I hadn't seen in decades. Returning to my motherland, Cambodia, after nearly fifty years, wasn't just about going back. It was about coming home – to the land, yes, but more than that, to a part of myself I had almost forgotten. If you've ever felt disconnected, unsure of where you truly belong, I want you to know, I've been there. And you're not alone.

There is something powerful that happens when we remember, not just in our minds, but in our soul and DNA. We begin to hear our own voice again. The distance, the silence, the pain – they don't erase our roots. They don't take away our right to belong. We carry our ancestor's history, our healing, and our hope. Together, we rise by reclaiming our culture, our stories, and our strength. We plant ourselves again with love, with pride, and with purpose.

So, if you are still searching, don't give up. If you're rebuilding, take your time. You are allowed to take up space. You're allowed to come home – to your truth, your identity, your roots. Your presence matters. You are enough. And the world is better because you are in it.

Chanthy Thong

94

To the beautiful souls who sometimes doubt themselves, life's challenges that present themselves each day are not meant to break us, but to push us forward, to awaken our inner strength and determination in this journey of life. We all deserve to live a life that feels good, one that matches the vison we hold in our hearts.

Rising above doubt and insecurities begins with our mindset. Our thoughts about everyday life need to be focused on the, *Yes, I can do this*. After all, *It is an inside job*. What we feel and allow into our mind and heart is our own choice. Finding that inner drive can be tough some days, but trust me, it is possible and worth every challenging thought and action. We don't have to change as a person, only tap into our courage and determination. Believing in ourselves is powerful; it will bring the most profound gifts to us that leave us wanting more.

Never doubt your ability to reach for your true desires that light up your heart. We are all worthy and capable. When you feel it in your heart, whatever your dream in life may be, you know it is possible. Visualising your desired life will ignite a fire within you. It will keep the passion alive and raise you above the doubt. We come together to rejoice in this life, all ultimately seeking the same thing: believing in ourselves and manifesting that abundant, delicious life we deserve.

Mary Crocker

95

Reflecting on ourselves is one of the hardest yet most rewarding challenges in life. Among the noise of the world, it can feel almost impossible to hear our own inner voice – yet that voice is where calm and clarity begin. Listening carefully helps us notice what we truly value, what we long for, and where we want to go. It reminds us that peace is not only an idea but a daily practice.

What I know for sure is that peace doesn't arrive all at once; it grows quietly when we create small moments of stillness. We can sit with a warm cup of tea and breathe deeply, write down our thoughts in a journal, or walk through trees and let the wind settle our minds. These simple habits teach us to meet ourselves with patience. From that gentle attention, kindness flows outward to friends, to strangers, and even to loved ones who live only in our memories.

Inner peace is not an illusion; it is a steady strength that allows us to hold both sadness and joy without losing balance. It gives us courage to face uncertainty, and it helps us see beauty even in difficult times. The voices of those who loved us echo inside, telling us that we belong, that we are never truly alone. Life keeps moving, but when we honour our inner voice, we can walk forward with lightness and hope.

Miyako Murayama

96

You are wise beyond measure. You are powerful. As you move through life, you are remembering – remembering the wisdom carried across lifetimes, remembering who you truly are. You are guided, protected, and never alone. You came to Earth with a plan. Every experience – pleasant or painful – was chosen to help you heal, grow, and expand. Before you arrived, you knew there would be challenges. Some people would push you; others would trigger you.

Yet every encounter was designed to awaken the fire within, to remind you of your inner power and strength. You came willingly, knowing the importance of your role in this great story. You are valuable. You are needed. The universe moves through you and responds to you. Every thought, feeling, word, and action carries energy that ripples outward, inspiring others. Your vibration is unique – there has never been and never will be another like you. You are a vital piece of the greater whole.

Remember, you are the universe, and the universe is you. You are loved, guided, and protected always. Keep your inner fire burning bright. Follow your inspiration, act on your inner calling, and trust the spark within you. When you do, the universe rises to meet you with synchronicity and magic. You are a creator. You are love in motion. You are here to inspire, to expand, and to remind others of their own brilliance. Stand tall. Shine bright. The world has been waiting for you.

Renata Grooby

97

Life's journey is filled with ups and downs, and grief and loss are inevitable stops along the way. Yet instead of getting stuck in the mud, you can choose to use these experiences as stepping-stones to growth and renewal. Take a deep breath. Wipe away your tears. Remember, every end marks a new beginning. Go gently with yourself and celebrate the small victories along the way. Give yourself permission to rest, to treat yourself, and to embrace moments of joy – because self-care is not selfish: it's essential.

Depression and struggle can feel like heavy burdens, but you are not alone. Begin with small practices that help shift your inner world: meditation, journalling, visualisation, or quiet self-reflection. These simple acts can help you gain clarity, rebuild confidence, and open space for healing. Reaching out for support – whether through self-help books, awareness groups, or trusted friends – is not weakness, but strength. When stress feels overwhelming, start with one small task. Even the smallest accomplishment can spark momentum and remind you of your capability. Journalling can be a powerful ally here: set gentle goals, start small, and let your words guide you toward the life you wish to create.

Most of all, remember to love yourself. Allow joy back into your days. Take on new projects, nurture your inner child, and make space for play. Healing is not about erasing the pain but about rediscovering your wholeness and remembering that life still holds beauty, purpose, and light.

Cynthia Haworth

98

I can feel it, something deep within me shifting. It's as if the whole world, both inside and out, is transforming. I know there will be upheavals, moments that feel chaotic, even cataclysmic, but I also know they will pass. Life will continue. And for the first time, I understand that my story isn't set in stone. I have the power to shape my reality, to create a life that aligns with who I truly am.

There's a collective awakening happening. I feel it in the air, in conversations, in the stillness. We're moving into something new, something softer, more genuine, a new way of being rooted in love, kindness, and compassion, not just for others, but for myself too. I came here for a reason. My soul chose this time, this place, this path. And I'll be honest; it hasn't been easy. The lessons have been heavy, often painful. But I'm starting to remember not just who I am, but *why* I'm here.

The Earth is shifting beneath our feet, literally and energetically, and I can feel that same tremble within me. It's a calling to align with a higher frequency, to return to source, to something ancient and powerful. There's an aliveness waking up inside me, something I hadn't felt in a long time. It's exhilarating, like remembering a dream I didn't know I forgot. And now I ask myself, *Am I ready? Am I willing to let go of the old stories and embrace this new way of being?* I think I am. I think I *must* – because everything I've ever been searching for has always been love.

Pauline Csuba

99

It's time to remind you about imagination. Imagination can be a guiding light, opening doors to new possibilities and enriching your experiences. In our early days of life, our imaginations are strong and vivid. Some of us had imaginary friends, and others would imagine what they would like to be when they grew up. Life seems to wear this down and can fade away as we grow up.

Our imagination can transport us to anywhere, be anyone, or just allow us to feel. In times of trouble, we can get our guidance by imagining what we need to do or say. When grief overwhelms us from the loss of a loved one, imagining they are sitting right there with you can bring a great sense of peace and calm.

Imagination is an inbuilt guiding system that just needs to be switched on. If you have trouble finding that switch, let's imagine right now where it could be, and turn it on. You are now ready to imagine anything. If something is troubling you right now, start imagining the outcome you feel you would like. The more you do this, the stronger your imagination muscle will grow. Imagination can break you free from rigid thinking, making life a more dynamic and fulfilling journey. The manifestation of our imagery is extremely powerful, so remember to flick the switch and just imagine.

Diana Anderson

100

You are enough. Yes, you. You are enough. We are in a time of deep societal and energetic change. Collectively, there is a need to tap into and lead from our soft courageous hearts to create a new world, one that is based on love, kindness, compassion, and connection. A world that allows our souls to shine, our children to play, and our hearts to stay open, flourish, and dream.

In this busy and chaotic world that glorifies bigger, better, more, this is your invitation to stop striving, to stop contorting yourself to be who you think you should be and accept your beautiful radiant self. You are not your mistakes, your guilt, or your past. You are a magical, brave, creative, and intuitive being. You are enough. You are more than enough. Know this to be the truth. When we know we are enough, when we feel the truth of our true value and worth in our bones without the need to prove our deserving, the world will change.

Put your hands on your heart, turn your attention within and connect with your beautiful heart. Know you are truly perfect in all your imperfections. Open the door to self-acceptance and self-love. Take a breath in and say out loud, "Today I am enough." Pause. Again, "Today I am enough." Pause. And again, "Today I am enough." How does that feel? The world needs your kindness and your powerfully soft, courageous heart. As do you. You are enough.

Debra Gillespie

101

Your heart is in a million pieces. Sometimes you feel you can't breathe. But here is hoping that others see and feel the wonderful, beautiful being that you miss so much, that one who was gone far too soon. Feeling their presence in all of our souls keeps us going. We are grateful they show up as a special part of our life and as angels. You might even say you shine through them and through them, *Love endures ALL things* (Corinthians 13:4).

Through these humble words, may others perceive the impact and the difference your lost ones made in many beautiful lives. Their support towards family, friends, and others was totally outstanding. Their heartfelt smile, their warm hugs, and their willingness to help and be there for others was always evident. Love of nature, sunshine, and the ocean are a beautiful reflection of their sweet soul.

When you find yourself thinking of your lost one, say this, *I thank you for allowing me to travel and share with you so many marvellous memories. You were here for a short period and not only left with your presence being noted, but for your absence to be heartfelt as well.* There are many rooms in the house of Our Father (John 12), and He had a room prepared for you. As you read this, let it sink into your soul, knowing that there will be a time when you will see your loved one again. Knowing this gives me some peace in my heart.

Mary Ann Trotter

102

If you are in an abusive relationship, or trying to leave one, please know this: you are not going crazy. It is not your fault. You are not broken. You will get through this. And you are definitely not alone. Leaving will be one of the hardest and bravest things you ever do. It will take all your strength and courage at a time when you feel emotionally, psychologically, and physically exhausted.

The decision to leave is the first step. Healing and the journey back to self is not simple or linear. The path winds and detours. It will lead you through rain and shine, over rugged mountains and into leafy valleys. Some steps may bring pain, but each one will carry purpose. Let yourself be open and the right people will join you – they will walk beside you, guiding you around the bends, through the storms, and across the rough terrain.

There will be flowers to smell along the way – moments of great beauty, blue skies, peaceful views, places to rest. On this journey, you will discover more about yourself than you ever imagined. You will realise how courageous, strong, and capable you are. You will allow yourself to be vulnerable and to trust again. You will appreciate the peace that comes from forgiveness, acceptance, and simplicity, that true growth rarely comes from comfort, and in that growth the real magic is found, giving yourself permission to step into the life your soul was born to live.

Donna Lea Turner

103

To the soul that is reading this, everything you need already exists inside of you. You are enough just as you are, just with being. You can do anything. You've got this. There's no need to push or do more. You are safe to be. Let the masks fall away, the expectations fade by your wayside. Look after yourself. Love yourself. Make yourself a priority, always.

Take yourself out on dates; be jolly, silly; have fun; be your biggest cheerleader. Let go of outside noise and expectations with ease. Be at peace. Be brave. Be courageous. Give yourself grace, particularly during trying times. After all, you're a spiritual being having a human experience. Remember when you are seeking clarity, go within, the answers you seek are there. Listen, be patient. They will come through.

I am grateful for it all – all the lessons, the good, the bad, and everything in between. It's all perspective and perception. Choose to see the lessons. Grow, learn and evolve through it all. Ask yourself, *What is the lesson here?* Sit with yourself, feel what you need to feel. Allow for the answers and clarity to flow in and through, without judgement or restriction. Be vulnerable and curious. Remember who you are: a powerful being, full of love, light, and wonder.

Louise (Lou) Nuttall

104

In your life journey, you will face many challenges, obstacles, and setbacks. People will doubt you, place limits on you, and even try to put you down. You will have doubting friends and family members. You may even have a doubting partner that criticises your ambition. These people will be present in your life should you aspire to achieving anything at all. From the Maths teacher, the pompous career advisor, the sceptical Martial Arts experts, to the business doubters, I realised that everything significant that I have ever achieved was preceded by someone saying I couldn't do it.

Of the many challenges you will face, however, self-doubt, in many ways, is the biggest dream-killer of all, because it is an inner battle that quietly operates, subconsciously, in the background. Conquer this, and you will push yourself forwards, achieve goals, and ultimately fulfil your potential; allow it to conquer you, and your dreams will remain just that. Dreams. Self-doubt will rob you of years and will rob you of living your best life. It must be exposed, dismantled, and defeated.

Overcome self-doubt and build up your self-belief and confidence by firstly increasing your self-awareness – knowing yourself – secondly, by starting to accumulate a catalogue of small wins which will serve as proof that you are who you tell yourself you are; and finally, by constantly speaking positively and encouragingly to yourself. If you follow these three steps, who knows what you can achieve?! Trust yourself. Believe in yourself. Have confidence in yourself.

Geoff Alexander

105

You have many unique qualities that make you a valuable part of this world. Yes, you! Yet you may question your place, feeling that quiet ache of wondering why anyone would want to stand beside you. I understand the weight of these thoughts; I've felt them too. It can feel like everyone else is worthy of love except us. But I also know that feeling unworthy, no matter how real it feels, does not make it true; even in our loneliest moments, love and support are often closer than we realise.

The truth is, love and support are not scarce resources, but abundant, always present, always waiting to reach us. Sometimes they arrive through the kindness of a friend, the presence of someone who listens, or the gentle guidance of a mentor. At other times, it's simply the comfort of knowing someone cares enough to stand near us while we overcome our latest life challenge. We don't need rescuing; we just need the courage to crack the armour we've built to protect ourselves to allow others in.

Perhaps the most powerful shift begins when we recognise that the compassion we long for already lives in us because we have been giving it away all along. Then, we begin to see that love flows both inward and outward, and in that flow, we find true belonging. Even when you feel lost, remember, you are never truly alone. Love will always find its way to you – if you let it.

Joanne Outram

106

Feeling unsure, scared, and alone in life can leave us feeling stuck and afraid to push forward. We can sit and feel unable to move through our pain. We feel we are the pain. It becomes us, the core of our identity. The truth is that our pain can be turned into our purpose. Through my own journey of being a two-time stage four cancer survivor, I know this to be true in every sense. Even when we are on our knees with what is or feels like a death sentence, up against a dark wall, this is where the power of change sits. We are not lost, for this is the place for where we are found: truly and profoundly found.

When you are in the maze of life, your mind might trick you into believing there is no way out, but there is always, always a way out. Before reacting or giving in, take the time to sit, stay grounded, breathe in deeply, recalibrate, and then start to think creatively about your new route. Then take the next step forward, no matter how small.

The essence of life is about being in the flow; it isn't about being in the fight. When we surrender to the stillness, we can listen for the answers we need to seek to create a new pathway. This is what turning up for ourselves is all about, ultimately leading us to the exit in the maze we had been lost in.

Karen Humphries

107

Do you know your medicine? In difficult times, we lean on something, someone, somewhere. Before it gets challenging, it can help to decide what you will draw strength from. But if you are already in the thick of it, just know that comfort can come in many forms. Choose wisely. Is it truly healing? In fact, if you can sit with your pain, face it, hear it speak its wisdom to you, and dig deep into your soul to find the part of you that can even love it, you will do well, my friend. You will be capable of miracles.

In this journey, not a single one of us will be left unmarked by sorrow of some sort. You are not alone. You are a part of this matrix we are co-creating together. What do you want to do with it now? Decide – because where attention goes, energy flows. Feel your feels. Cry your tears. Scream your screams. Then look in the mirror and remind yourself you are good enough. Affirm what you deserve. Set an intention that aligns with your most authentic self. And then make a plan and take action.

Let the universe open the doors and say yes to your desires. Go for it! I dare you. And when you look back, let the only words be *Thank you* for a past you lived to the best of your ability. And your best is good enough. Be your cure. Let it be miraculous!

Kea Evangelista

108

To the beautiful lost soul who is feeling a mess, broken-hearted, and deeply emotional, unconfident, shy and silent for words, I get you and I know you can heal your life with change and transformation of your mindset. How? By believing in you! You are strength! You can design and plan your vision and future life by taking the first step to achieving your calling. When you're ready with inner confidence and strength, you can find your inner freedom.

We can change with travel! This opens your eyes! The world is your oyster! You can develop and inspire yourself with knowledge, reading books, self-help, and taking courses! Your open mind will give you the insight and determination you need to achieve your success. Your powerful mind, intuition, and heart will take you to places of destiny within. The universe and your faith will guide you every day. You are connected to nature and abundance. Honour your life and yourself as it's a gift.

You are a sparkle of love to yourself and others. You are the enlightened flame shining bright light to the world. You are a leader of light! A star! Your angels are guiding and supporting you. I believe in you, and you must believe in yourself. You can do this! Make time for nature and, with growth, like a flower, you will bloom. You are precious and rare. Be grateful every day! Love your life and it will love you back. Connect and ignite your powerful energy and empower yourself. Wishing you happiness.

Michelle Webb

109

If you feel you are in the darkness right now, know that you are supported, loved, and guided every step of the way. But promise me this: do not give up on yourself. These are the moments that reveal your brilliance, your resilience, and your strength, to re-create a life that is full and meaningful to you.

One day, you will walk this path again. You will see, hear, and feel your growth and transformation. You will witness many new beginnings, each one tracing back to the moments of your darkest hours, when you felt vulnerable, insecure, and shy. It was in those moments that you chose to listen deeply to your heart and soul, and you felt your way back to the light. You trusted and believed in yourself knowing that you had a divine place, purpose, and belonging in the world.

One day, you will be the guiding light for others. Though this place may feel uncomfortable now, trust that you are finding your way through the darkness, becoming the person you were born to be. Remember those sacred moments, when you listened deeply within and heard the whispers of the ancestors, spiritual guides, or your own deep inner knowing. These voices have always been with you, gently guiding you through the challenges. Hold closely the places etched in memory where fear, doubt, and uncertainty fell away, and you chose to believe, love, and trust in yourself. These are the moments that shaped your spirit and revealed your capacity for greatness – moments of inner strength, when you witnessed your true self emerging from within.

Karen Reys

110

When a relationship ends, the pain can feel like a devastating jolt. Your heart aches, your world shifts, and you may feel lost in a sea of emotion. It's natural to look back and wonder about the choices you made – the moments that led you together and the ones that pulled you apart. But here's a truth to hold onto: every relationship, no matter how it ends, was a step in your becoming.

You took a risk by opening your heart. That choice was not a mistake – it was courage. It means you dared to love, to hope, and to grow. The ending doesn't erase the meaning or the beauty that once was. Instead, it invites you to reconnect with yourself – to rediscover the parts of you that may have been quiet while love took centre stage.

Healing takes time. Some days, you'll miss them. Other days, you'll glimpse your strength and feel a quiet pride for making it through. Surround yourself with people who remind you who you are and allow yourself to feel everything without judgement. And when hope begins to stir again, don't silence it. Hope is not denial; it's the gentle whisper that life still has love waiting for you – perhaps in someone new, but always within yourself first. You are not broken. You are rebuilding. And this is not the end – it's the beginning of a new kind of love story: the one where you learn to love yourself again.

David Vine

111

For the quiet introverted person staying in the shadows, afraid to be seen and heard, I feel for you as I, too, have been there. Hiding ourselves to avoid the fears of feeling unsafe, being judged or hurt, of making mistakes, or feeling not good enough and not loved. Staying silent because we are afraid of saying the wrong thing or voicing our wants and needs for fear of rejection. The feeling of loneliness that sits in the background and the longing for something we feel we do not deserve or appears always just out of reach.

You do not need to stay trapped in your fears. They are not who you are; they are just the shadows that you choose to stand in until you step out of them. Your true self, the loving, compassionate, joyful, and adventurous soul that you are, is waiting behind the fear to shine its light. I know you can be that person. You have so much untapped courage within you to make the choices, to become strong in who you are, unafraid of what others think or what might happen, and confident to speak out about your needs, dreams, and desires.

Imagine your life if you were able to be everything you feel you are not. Believe that such a change is possible and allow yourself to let it happen. So come out of the shadows and into the light, without fear, and reclaim yourself to live life to the fullest.

Sue Newport

Conclusion

It is my deepest wish that within the pages of this book you have found not just one, but many messages that have moved your heart. I hope that you have felt the love of each of the co-authors who took the time to write a contribution with the prayer and intention that it might uplift or touch your life at the right moment. They wrote for you because, like me, they believe that you are extraordinary and that you deserve to thrive during your time on Earth.

May you keep this special book on your desk or bedside table and continue to pick it up and open to a random page when you need a moment of inspiration. May it be a reminder that you are never alone in this life, no matter what it is that you are facing, and that you are *loved*. And may you always be guided on your journey, as you always have been, as you strive to do what you were born to do and live the extraordinary life that I believe you were born for.

Greater possibilities are ready and waiting for you – so claim them.

Healing is possible – so allow it.

A brighter future can be yours – so live it.

With all my love and inspiration,

Emily Gowor

Acknowledgements

I wish to thank the following people from my heart for their contribution in bringing this beautiful book to life. Firstly, to my dear friend, Hamish Withington, for our deep conversation in early 2025 when the vision and idea for the book project first appeared in my mind. Without you and our deep conversations, this book and the inspiring journey it has taken us on would never have happened.

Secondly, I would love to thank each and every one of the co-authors who believed in the vision for the book and who came together to share their wisdom and inspiration with the readers. From Panama to Portugal and beyond, you are truly an inspiring global collective of extraordinary individuals from many walks of life, and your messages are appreciated. Thank you for your effort, devotion, and love in making this book a reality.

My heartfelt gratitude to Kim Guthrie for being an amazing second-in-command and assistant project manager for *Words That Change The World*. Your beautiful heart, brilliant mind, and grounded energy have been an asset in this project, to say the least. Thank you for your service of love in reviewing the submissions and supporting the co-authors to share their messages and for being my formidable teammate in this inspiring venture.

To my close friends and loved ones who encouraged me along the way and supported the vision of this book as it came to life: Michael Bromley, Hamish Withington, Maryke Prinsloo, and Anne Fry. You are true legends in my life, and I love you.

Thank you to my publishing team for your outstanding work. Yet again, you have helped me to release a truly inspiring book for humanity. To the designer who captured my vision with the book cover design, to Ursula McCabe for the editing, and to Chandrashekar Yadav for another beautiful book layout, to my designer Noel for finalising the book cover for print, and to the rest of my publishing team within Gowor International Publishing. I appreciate you deeply. Thank you!

Contact The Co-Authors

If you felt moved by one or two pieces in the book, my invitation is to reach out to the co-author to let them know that their message touched your life!

You can find their contact details below:

1: Hamish Withington – www.hamishwho.com.au

2: Heidi Goodman – www.mindsconnect.com.au

3: Barbie Cawthan – www.crystalnpearlco.com

4: Lena Banzer – www.substack.com/@lenabanzer

5: Pat Armistead – www.patarmitstead.com

6: Faith Monteverde – info@emilygowor.com

7: Alan Jackson – www.alanjackson.me

8: Michele Peppler – www.michelepeppler.com

9: Karin Golisch – www.aboutunow.com

10: Karen Hepi – info@emilygowor.com

11: Maryke Prinsloo – www.outbackmigration.com.au

12: Vonny Mullins – www.facebook.com/vonny.mullins

13: Kim Guthrie – www.kimguthrie.com.au

14: Maureen Callister – www.maureencallister.com

15: Nicole Masseque – www.simplyamazing.co

16: Kellie-Ann Smith – www.facebook.com/kellie.smith.948494

17: Ed Breedveld – www.facebook.com/DutchyBear

18: Myrah Moon – www.facebook.com/profile.php?id=61579914953245

19: Shanelle Anderson-Cooper – www.isee-you.com.au

20: Angelika Jankovic – info@emilygowor.com

21: Trina Ghauri – www.myspaceofpossibility.com

22: Veronica Jackson – info@emilygowor.com

23: Dr Laraib Malik – info@emilygowor.com

24: Katharine Cheetham – www.facebook.com/katharine.cheetham.3

25: Michael Gould – info@emilygowor.com

26: Christine Maudy – www.livinginspired.com.au

27: Britt Brennan – www.brittbrennan.com.au

28: Haley Jones – www.drhaleyjones.com.au

29: Maria Gallagher – www.instagram.com/mg_art88

31: Adam James – www.instagram.com/adamjamesfun

32: Jenni Albrecht – info@emilygowor.com

33: Tracy Knibbs – www.tracyknibbs.com

34: Manjila Shrestha – www.instagram.com/enlightening_with_destination

35: Alexandra Lange Bernal – www.martha-and-alexandra.com

36: Kate Taylor – info@emilygowor.com

37: Colin Lee – www.inspirerealty.com

38: Zenith Dunstan – www.zenithdunstan.com

39: Patricia Frederick – info@emilygowor.com

40: Di Kersey – www.isnteverythingclear.com

41: Anna Willey – www.annnawilleyinternational.com

42: Jeanette Cousins – www.facebook.com/jeanette.cousins.925

43: Yvonne Thompson – www.facebook.com/profile.php?id=100085578429682

44: Lance Garbutt – www.lanceg6.wixsite.com/lancegarbutt

45: Sandy Hanrahan – www.wildheartsbusiness.com

46: Allison Thomas – www.allythomas.com.au

47: Charlie Hovenden – info@emilygowor.com

48: Phillip Manfredi – www.phillipmanfredi.com

49: Lyndy Saltmarsh – www.renewyou.com.au

50: Claudia Ehler – www.charlieh.com.au

51: Codey Orgill – www.codeyorgill.com

52: Emily Gowor – www.emilygowor.com

53: Michael Bromley – www.michaelbromley.com.au

54: Anne Fry – www.annefry.au

55: Yvonne Haeaefke – www.insightfulout.co

56: Sheilla Ann Kennedy – www.sheila-kennedy.com

57: Emily Robinson – www.bio.site/ipikproject

58: Claudia Lopez – info@emilygowor.com

59: Paul Morris Segal – www.facebook.com/PaulMorrisSegal1

60: Emilia Bruckner – www.facebook.com/emilia.brucknerau

61: Shenice Portelli – info@emilygowor.com

62: Nita Joy – www.instagram.com/nitajoy2

63: Jay Harris – www.jayharris.com.au

64: Jan McIntyre – www.instagram.com/janmcintyre2020

65: Ursula McCabe – info@emilygowor.com

66: Robert Grimes – www.lovelifematters.com.au

67: Deborah Stathis – www.facebook.com/deborahstathis.author.speaker.coach

68: Melanie McKane – info@emilygowor.com

69: Kate Sanders – info@emilygowor.com

70: Theresa Grainger – www.instagram.com/theresajanegrainger

71: Angela Peris – www.angelaperis.com

72: Rosalind Sansbury – www.facebook.com/rosalindsansburyawakeninghumanitysheart

73: Jacqui Hartley-Smith – www.instagram.com/positive.solutions

74: Tracey Gordon – www.agilelearningsolutionsau.org

75: Dr Kim Jobst – www.constelos.com

76: Melanie Mayell – www.thecreatrix.co.nz

77: Dr Kathrine Harrison – www.embodiedalchemy.com.au

78: Lana Arvidson – www.flickresults.com.au

79: Diana Hansen – www.dianahansen.com

80: Annie Chandler – info@emilygowor.com

81: Emme Krystelle – info@emilygowor.com

82: Martha Bernal – www.martha-and-alexandra.com

83: Jane Gruebner – www.themasterkeyspath.com

84: Suzanne Fox-Kennedy – www.facebook.com/reikihealingwithsuzanne

85: Tim Matcham – www.timmatcham.com

86: Honor Turner – info@emilygowor.com

87: Alison Pilling – www.alipilling.com

88: Niki Rentoul – https://linktr.ee/nikirentoul

89: Dimitra Mersinia – www.linkedin.com/in/dimitra-mersinia-97104944

90: Bianca Madison-Vuleta – www.effectivehealthsolutions.org

91: Janelle Fletcher – www.janellefletcher.com

92: Jenny Kjaer – www.alexawritesitallaway.blogspot.com

93: Chanthy Thong – www.intohealthbeautywellness.com

94: Mary Crocker – info@emilygowor.com

95: Miyako Murayama – info@emilygowor.com

96: Renata Grooby – www.renatagrooby.com

97: Cynthia Haworth – www.counsellingthatworks.com

98: Pauline Csuba – www.creativetheta.com.au

99: Diana Anderson – info@emilygowor.com

100: Debra Gillespie – www.debragillespie.com

101: Mary Ann Trotter – info@emilygowor.com

102: Donna Lea Turner – www.donnaleaturner.com

103: Louise (Lou) Nuttall – www.enrichingcollective.com.au

104: Geoff Alexander – info@emilygowor.com

105: Joanna Outram – www.empowermenteditions.com

106: Karen Humphries – www.karenhumphries.com.au

107: Kea Evangelista – www.facebook.com/profile.php?id=61579971965521

108: Michelle Webb – info@emilygowor.com

109: Karen Reys – www.ceedhealing.com.au

110: David Vine – info@emilygowor.com

111: Sue Newport – info@emilygowor.com

About The Author

Emily Gowor is a self-help writer, author, speaker and the visionary behind the *Words That Change The World* book.

After overcoming near-suicidal depression earlier in her journey, Emily turned her life around and devoted herself and her life to inspiring people to reach for more. She has now spent more than 18 years helping people to achieve their goals and dreams.

As the author of 14 books on the topics of self-help, purpose, potential, and writing – including *The Life You Dream Of*, *Born Great*, and *Reflections on Purpose* – Emily produced an award-winning blog, attracting thousands of readers. Emily has spoken on stage in Australia and internationally, sharing the stage with leaders including Dr. John Demartini, global best-selling author and star of *The Secret*.

Emily's life's work and presence has touched thousands of lives globally over the past 20 years. Her life-changing programs and 1-1 mentoring guide inspire people to create the life they love and fulfil their purpose on Earth. Extensively trained in human behaviour and psychology, Emily is Master Certified in Neuro-Linguistic Programming, as well as being a previously trained facilitator in the life-changing work of Dr John Demartini.

As a winner of the 2012 & 2014 Anthill 30 under 30 Young Entrepreneur Award, Emily's diverse entrepreneurial journey has included founding and running a publishing company for 10 years, speaking and training, generating 6-figure revenues in her business for more than a decade, hosting 7-day retreats, and working with people and leaders across many arenas. Her ongoing mission is to inspire, guide, and uplift people to achieve their dreams and make their meaningful impact on humanity.

Emily has been featured in the media sharing her messages of encouragement and wisdom, including her appearance on the *Global Women Empowerment* TV show for Channel 31 in Melbourne, Australia. Having fulfilled and created a profound and thriving career helping people achieve their dreams, Emily continues to inspire people from around the world to reach for more in life.

www.emilygowor.com